What Are They Saying About Mark?

Frank J. Matera

PAULIST PRESS
New York / Mahwah

Library of Congress Cataloging-in-Publication Data

Matera, Frank J.
    What are they saying about Mark?

    Bibliography: p.
    1. Bible. N.T. Mark—Criticism, interpretation,
etc.—History—20th century. I. Title.
BS2585.2.M294   1987   226'.306'0904   87-2353
ISBN 0-8091-2885-3 (pbk.)

Published by Paulist Press
997 Macarthur Boulevard
Mahwah, N.J. 07430

Printed and bound in the
United States of America

Contents

For my parents
on the occasion of their fiftieth wedding anniversary
1937–1987

Acknowledgements

I wish to acknowledge the help and assistance of two colleagues in the preparation of this manuscript—Father John Galvin, Professor of Systematic Theology at Saint John's Seminary, Brighton, and Father Laurence McGrath, Librarian at Saint John's. Father Galvin read most of the manuscript in its early stages and, as always, provided insightful comments. Father McGrath proofread the entire manuscript and, as usual, offered important suggestions for improving the work. To both I owe a debt of gratitude.

Abbreviations

ZNW	Zeitschrift für die neutestamentliche Wissenshaft
NTS	New Testament Studies
Int	Interpretation
JR	Journal of Religion
SBLDS	Society of Biblical Literature Dissertation Series
JBL	Journal of Biblical Literature
RB	Revue biblique
BETL	Bibliotheca ephemeridum theologicarum lovaniensium
JAAR	Journal of the American Academy of Religion
	Unless otherwise noted, scriptural quotations are from the Revised Standard Version of the Bible.

Introduction

The title of this book *What Are They Saying About Mark?* should be self-explanatory to most readers. It is a brief survey of what New Testament scholars have been saying about the Gospel according to Mark for the past twenty to twenty-five years. The purpose of the book is not to open new territory in Markan studies but to introduce others to the lay of the land.

Anyone well acquainted with Markan scholarship knows that the secondary literature about this Gospel has grown to such proportions that even those professionally engaged in Markan studies find it difficult, if not impossible, to master. Thus I hope that this volume will prove of some assistance to those beginning their study of Mark's Gospel. If they can discover where others have been, it will be easier for them to mark out their own path.

Given the size of this book and the abundance of monographs and articles on Mark's Gospel, the reader will understand that the present volume makes no claim at being an exhaustive study. What I have attempted is an introduction to some important areas of Markan scholarship which involve questions both theological and methodological. In doing so I have chosen from works written in German and French as well as English in order to alert the reader that the study of Mark's Gospel has long since become an international affair. Undoubtedly those engaged in Markan scholarship will point to the absence of this or that work and question

the choices I have made. I welcome their critique; such criticism
is legitimate and to be expected.

Although I do not agree with the positions of all the authors
represented in this volume, I have learned from these scholars and
have tried to present their views as objectively as possible. For the
most part I have limited my own critical comments to the brief
conclusions which end each chapter and to the conclusion of this
book, but undoubtedly the reader will detect my biases throughout
this work.

If there is some orginality in this book, it is my attempt to
make sense of what is happening in Markan studies. As the reader
will soon discover, despite the impressive work done upon Mark's
Gospel, there remains a number of strong divisions among interpreters. Although there is no end to hypotheses and new methodological approaches, I do not think it is possible to speak either
of a consensus in Markan studies or of any clear direction in the
present situation. Mark's Gospel remains as challenging and elusive today as it may have seemed nearly two thousand years ago.
It is this elusive quality which continues to intrigue new genera-
tions of interpreters.

The movement of this book is simple. It begins with a brief
survey of the setting for Mark's Gospel. Where was it written?
What was the nature of the community for which it was written?
What were the circumstances surrounding its writing?

The second and third chapters deal with the central theological concerns of Mark's Gospel: Christology and discipleship. In
recent years these have been the most lively topics of conversation
among Markan scholars. The flow of erudite articles and monographs dealing with them shows no sign of abating. Scholars are
still asking about Mark's conception of Jesus' person as well as
his view of the disciples and discipleship.

The fourth and fifth chapters are concerned with questions
which are more methodological in nature. How was Mark's Gospel composed? What sources did the evangelist employ? How can

they be detected? What is the nature of Mark's narrative? Does it correspond to any known genre in the Greco-Roman world? How do we read Mark as story today?

My own interest in the Gospel of Mark began nearly twenty-five years ago when I was a seminarian at the American College at the University of Louvain. Since that time I have never tired of this Gospel, and, far from mastering it, I have discovered that it continues to master me. I hope that this brief survey will introduce another generation to a Gospel perennially new.

1
The Setting for Mark's Gospel

Introduction

New Testament (NT) scholars distinguish three stages in the growth of the Gospels: the very words and deeds of the historical Jesus, a period of oral transmission, and the writings of the evangelists.[1] In order to investigate each of these stages, scholars have employed specific methodologies. For example, those interested in the words and deeds of Jesus must deal with the question of sources. What are the sure and reliable sources for constructing a life of Jesus? This is the question of source criticism. Those concerned about the period of oral transmission (the time between Jesus' death and the first written Gospel) must ask how the oral traditions were preserved and handed down in the early Church. This is the question of form criticism. Finally, those who want to know the evangelist's theology and point of view must ask how the evangelist arranges and modifies his material. This is the question of redaction criticism. Each stage in the growth of the Gospels, therefore, has a corresponding methodology.

Life of Jesus	—	Source Criticism
Oral Tradition	—	Form Criticism
The Evangelists	—	Redaction Criticism

In addition to these three stages, NT scholars speak of various life settings against which the Gospel material can be studied. There is the life setting of the historical Jesus, the life setting of the early Church, and the life setting of the evangelists and their communities. Again, source, form and redaction criticism investigate each of these life settings.

Source Criticism	—	the life setting of Jesus
Form Criticism	—	the life setting of the early Christian community
Redaction Criticism	—	the life setting of the evangelist's community

In recent years Markan scholarship has been most interested in the third of these settings: the life setting of Mark the evangelist and the community for which he wrote.[2] Aware that each evangelist addressed a specific community, scholars inquire about the various communities or churches reflected in the NT.[3] In the case of the Gospels, they seek to determine the settings for which the evangelists composed their works. This inevitably results in questions about time and place, but it also involves other questions. What was the makeup of the evangelist's community? Was it Jewish Christian, Gentile Christian or both? What problems did the community face? Were there internal problems of leadership and belief or external difficulties such as persecution? The answers to these and other questions lead to a hypothetical portrait of the community for which the evangelist wrote. Since any literature is most profitably read when the reader understands something of its background, a knowledge of a Gospel's life setting can be helpful for a deeper appreciation of its message and the author's accomplishment.

In this chapter we shall review several hypotheses concerning the setting for Mark's Gospel. These proposals necessarily deal with the questions of time and place. In the case of Mark, the fundamental choices are simple. Was the Gospel written before or after the Jewish war and the destruction of Jerusalem (70 A.D.)? Was the Gospel written in Rome, by an "interpreter" of Peter, or was it composed by an unknown Christian in either Galilee or Syria?

Mark the Interpreter of Peter

In the case of the Gospel according to Mark, there is a rich vein of patristic evidence which testifies that Mark was the interpreter of Peter and that the Gospel was composed at Rome.[4] The pride of place belongs to a quotation from Papias, the bishop of Hierapolis in Asia Minor. The quotation is found in *The History of the Church* by Eusebius (263–339). Eusebius quotes from a section of an otherwise lost work of Papias, *Exegesis of the Lord's Oracles* (about A.D. 140). In the quotation, Papias himself cites the words of an elder named John who says that Mark was the interpreter of Peter.

> This, too, the presbyter used to say, "Mark, who had been Peter's interpreter, wrote down carefully, but not in order, all that he remembered of the Lord's sayings and doings. For he had not heard the Lord or been one of His followers, but later, as I said, one of Peter's. Peter used to adapt his teaching to the occasion, without making a systematic arrangement of the Lord's sayings, so that Mark was quite justified in writing down some things just as he remembered them. For he had one purpose only—to leave out nothing that he had heard, and to make no misstatement about it."[5]

The quotation has produced no end to scholarly debate. What does the elder mean by calling Mark the "interpreter" of Peter?

Where do the words of the elder end and those of Papias begin? Who is the Mark to whom the elder refers?

Despite these difficulties, until recently most scholars accepted the major point of Papias' testimony: there is a connection between the author of the Gospel and Peter.

In addition to Papias' witness, the patristic evidence includes the following.

- A remark by Justin Martyr concerning "Peter's memoirs" which may be a reference to Mark's Gospel (*Dialogue with Trypho*, 106).
- A statement by Irenaeus that Mark "the disciple and interpreter of Peter" wrote after the deaths of Peter and Paul (*Against Heresies*, 3.1.1.).
- An anti-Marcionite Prologue which says that Mark was "Peter's interpreter," and that he wrote in the regions of Italy after the death of Peter.
- A statement by Clement of Alexandria who says that Mark "a companion of Peter" wrote during Peter's lifetime at the urging of the people of Rome where Peter preached (Eusebius, *The History of the Church*, vi. 14. 6–7).
- A statement by Origen that the Gospel of Mark was written by Mark as Peter instructed him (Eusebius, *The History of the Church*, vi. 25. 5).
- A comment by Jerome that Mark "the interpreter of the Apostle Peter" was the first bishop of Alexandria in Egypt. (*Commentary on Matthew, Prooemium*, 6)

From one point of view, the patristic evidence is overwhelming, and it is not surprising that scholars have employed it to determine the setting for the Gospel. But it is also clear that there is a certain "growth" in the tradition which begins with Mark as Peter's interpreter and then moves to locating the Gospel in Rome, first after Peter's death and then before Peter's death, thereby granting it greater apostolic approbation. Furthermore, scholars have questioned if the various witnesses represent independent traditions, or if they all have their origin in Papias' testimony. The constant reference to Mark as Peter's interpreter suggests the latter.

An article by Kurt Niederwimmer on the authorship of the Second Gospel[6] challenges the trustworthiness of Papias' testimony and the traditional position that the author of the Gospel is the John Mark mentioned in the Acts of the Apostles (see Acts 12:12).

As for Papias, Niederwimmer argues that his testimony is a pure literary fiction developed by Papias in his struggle against the Gnostics of Asia Minor in the second century. Papias no more knew who the real author of the Gospel was than did his alleged informant, John the elder. Niederwimmer claims that Papias, taking a clue from 1 Peter 5:13 ("She who is at Babylon, who is likewise chosen, sends you greetings; so does *my son Mark*"), developed this testimony to give this Gospel the apostolic authority of Peter in order to enhance its value against the Gnostics who had their own gospels.

As for the author of the Gospel, Niederwimmer doubts that it was the Jerusalem Christian, John Mark, whose mother Mary had a house in Jerusalem (Acts 12:12). The author of this Gospel is not sufficiently familiar with the geography of Palestine (see 7:31 where the evangelist implies that Tyre is north of Sidon), nor is he intimately acquainted with Jewish practices (see 7:3–4 which seems to be written from the point of view of a non-Jew). Moreover, since the stories regarding Peter show the same characteristics as other stories in the Gospel, Niederwimmer judges that they do not derive from the apostle. Thus, the author of the Gospel was not the "interpreter" of Peter but an unknown Gentile Christian who wrote specifically for Gentiles in the west.

The recent work of Martin Hengel, *Studies in the Gospel of Mark*,[7] stands in sharp contrast to the positions adopted by Niederwimmer and others. Hengel is aware that contemporary scholarship tends to dismiss Papias' testimony as "a secondary, apologetic vindication of the apostolic origin of the Second Gospel,"[8] but he argues that it represents the critical comments of one who esteemed the oral tradition as more important than written words. The Papias tradition cannot be a literary invention because the connection between Peter and Mark is independently attested in 1 Peter 5:13. Therefore, Hengel maintains that Papias received his testimony from John the elder whose activity should be dated about 70–100 A.D.

As for the author's relationship to Peter, Hengel notes that in addition to Papias it is independently attested to by Justin Martyr who refers to the reminiscences of Peter (*Dial.* 106. 3). In Hengel's estimation, the best explanation that the Gospel according to Mark survived, despite the fact that Matthew employed about ninety percent of it in his own Gospel, is that from the beginning the work of Mark was "bound up with the authority of the name of Peter."[9]

In Hengel's view, "Mark was a Greek-speaking Jewish Christian who also understood Aramaic."[10] The numerous Aramaic or Hebrew words and formulae of the Gospel (3:17–19; 5:41; 7:11; 8:34; 10:46; 11:9–10; 14:1,32,36,45; 15:22,34) convince him that Mark was not a Gentile Christian even though he presumably writes for Gentiles. Although Mark is unfamiliar with Galilee, he is acquainted with Jerusalem and Palestinian Judaism. Therefore, Hengel identifies him with the John Mark of Acts, a former inhabitant of Jerusalem.

Finally, in an interesting study of the titles of the Gospels, Hengel offers ancillary evidence that a Christian named Mark composed the Gospel which bears his name. Noticing that the form of the Gospel titles ("The Gospel according to Mark," etc.) was already fixed before the close of the second century, Hengel deduces that the titles are not late products of the second century but can be traced to the time of the Gospels (69–100). Practical necessities such as the reading of Scripture in worship, the exchange of books between communities and the growth of community libraries and book-chests would have made it necessary to identify the author of a particular work. Hengel conjectures that the title "The Gospel according to Mark" may have been given to the Gospel by the authority who copied the Gospel as early as 69 A.D. If this is the case, then the name Mark points to the original author.

Mark a Roman Gospel

Scholars who support a Roman origin for Mark's Gospel have developed a number of theories to explain the setting in which the evangelist wrote. These scholars usually acknowledge that Mark was addressing Gentile Christians sometime shortly before or after the destruction of Jerusalem and its temple by the Romans in 70 A.D. Here chapter thirteen, Jesus' apocalyptic discourse, plays an important role since it reveals an atmosphere in which Christian apocalypticism (lively hope that the endtime is about to occur and that Jesus, the Son of Man, will soon return) plays an important role and in which persecution has begun, or is about to begin.

Martin Hengel argues that Mark 13 does not presuppose the catastrophe of 70 A.D. Rather, he sees the evangelist writing at a time shortly after the community's loss of its great leaders (Peter and Paul) through martyrdom. It is a period in which the community is in danger of being leaderless and apocalyptic expectation is threatening to run out of control.

For Hengel such a situation is most understandable in the great year of terror, 69 A.D. The years immediately prior to 69 can be described as apocalyptic in character. In 64 Nero persecuted the Christians of Rome, and among those martyred were Peter and Paul. Toward the end of Nero's reign, there were reports of famine and unrest. In 66 the Jewish war began, a war which ended in 70 with the destruction of Jerusalem and its temple. In 68, after Nero's suicide, there was a bloody civil war in which three emperors lost their lives (Galba, Otho, Vitellius). Not only was there unrest in Rome, there was rebellion abroad. Add to these political facts the earthquakes that Italy experienced in 68, and it is not difficult to understand why the Christians of Rome would have viewed the events prior to 70 as signs of the endtime.

Hengel maintains that this is the atmosphere in which Mark the evangelist writes. The temple of Jerusalem has not yet been destroyed, but the author can see that the event is at hand. He expects the appearance of the antichrist in the sanctuary of Jerusalem's temple. Hengel interprets this antichrist, mentioned in Mark 13:14 ("the desolating sacrilege"), as Nero come back to life. When this event occurs, the final stages of the messianic woes will be initiated, and then the Son of Man will return.

Ernest Best also contends that Mark wrote before the destruction of Jerusalem. In *Mark The Gospel as Story*[11] he suggests that Mark's community "was in danger of slipping back into 'the easy and self-indulgent life which seemed to be the goal of the Greco-Roman world.' "[12] According to Best, the temptations mentioned in Jesus' explanation of the parable of the sower (4:10–20) were real for the members of Mark's community, and the community feared further persecution. While the community is concerned with apocalyptic hope, perhaps as a way of avoiding persecution, Mark calls it to take up the cross. So the evangelist acts as a pastor to a community which has lost its original fervor.

In distinction to these theories, which propose that the Gospel was composed in the aftermath of Nero's persecution and before the destruction of Jerusalem, is the thesis of S.G. Brandon. For several years he has argued that Mark was written in the aftermath of the Jewish war as an *apologia* for Roman Christians.

In *Jesus and the Zealots*[13] Brandon sets a date shortly after 71 A.D. for the Gospel's composition. In the year 71 the Roman Christians would have seen the great procession celebrating

Rome's victory over the Jews. In that procession, described by the Jewish historian Josephus (*Wars of the Jews,* vii, 116–157), the Romans even displayed "the purple hangings of the sanctuary," that is, the temple curtain mentioned in Mark 15:38. In Brandon's view, this visual display of triumph would have affected the Roman Christians in two ways. First, it reminded them that their own faith "stemmed from this Jewish people who had so fiercely revolted against Roman rule."[14] Second, it confronted them "with the serious possibility that they might be regarded . . . as being themselves infected with Jewish revolutionary ideas."[15] Against this background, Mark wrote the Gospel to explain Pilate's condemnation of Jesus as a revolutionary, i.e., the "King of the Jews."

In composing the Gospel, Mark explains this embarrassing fact by shifting the responsibility for the death of Jesus to the Jewish authorities. But Mark, according to Brandon, was not content with the theme of Jewish responsibility. Throughout the Gospel the evangelist also develops the themes that although Jesus was a Jew, he was not appreciated by his own, and "he implicitly repudiated his racial relationships with the Jews."[16] Furthermore, Jesus' own disciples understood him as the Jewish Messiah, but they did not accept him as the divine Savior of mankind. So Brandon interprets the Gospel of Mark as consistently denigrating the Jewish leaders and people, the family of Jesus and his original apostles, thereby dissociating the Roman Christians from Jewish revolutionary activity.

The climax of the Gospel comes with the tearing of the temple curtain (15:38) and the confession of the Roman centurion that Jesus was truly the Son of God (15:39). The tearing of the curtain indicates that Judaism has been superseded by a nobler faith, and the centurion's confession presages the Gentiles' acceptance of Jesus as the Son of God.[17]

Not all authors who situate Mark's Gospel in Rome explain its setting in terms of threatening persecution either before or after

the fall of Jerusalem. Benoit Standaert judges that Mark wrote
after the destruction of Jerusalem, but in his view the setting for
the Gospel is the liturgy of the Roman Church.

In *L'Évangile selon Marc: Composition et Genre Litteraire*[18]
Standaert develops the hypothesis that the Gospel was read as a
Christian paschal Haggadah (narrative or story) on the vigil (Sat-
urday–Sunday) after the fourteenth day of the Jewish month Nisan
(Passover). The purpose of this reading was to introduce new adherents of the faith to the rite of baptism which was conferred in
the morning (Easter).

To support his thesis, Standaert points to baptismal and paschal imagery in the Gospel. The prologue of the Gospel (1:1–13),
for example, begins with a call by John to baptism and conversion, a promise that Jesus will baptize with the Holy Spirit, and
the example of Jesus' own baptism. That Jesus does not baptize
with the Holy Spirit during the Gospel story suggests to Standaert
that the call to baptism and this promise are directed to the Gospel's listeners at the Easter vigil.

Standaert claims that there is further baptismal imagery at the
conclusion of the Gospel in the person of the young man who flees
naked at Jesus' arrest (14:51). Another young man, "dressed in a
white robe" (16:5), appears at the empty tomb "very early on the
first day of the week" (16:2) to announce the resurrection. For
Standaert the appearance of these young men should be understood in terms of baptismal imagery. Thus there is a symmetry
between the prologue in which John the Baptist announces the
coming of Jesus and the epilogue where a young man points to
Galilee as the place that the risen Lord will appear to the disciples.
Both John and the young man point to baptism.

Standaert also sees baptismal and paschal imagery within the
Gospel story. For example, when James and John ask for the seats
of honor at Jesus' right and left, Jesus inquires if they are able to
be baptized with the baptism with which he is to be baptized
(10:38). At the Last Supper Peter and the disciples proclaim, "If

I must die with you, I will not deny you'' (14:31). For those about to be baptized, these words would have served as an explanation of what participation in the Eucharist entails. One who is baptized with Jesus and eats at the eucharistic table must be prepared to die with him.

Finally, Standaert points to the eschatological atmosphere of the Gospel (8:39–9:1; 13:1–37; 14:62). This eschatological hope suggests that the community read the Gospel with the fervent conviction that the return of Jesus, as the Son of Man, was imminent.

According to Standaert, then, the setting for Mark's Gospel is the Easter vigil celebrated at Rome. The Gospel was read in its entirety, at a single sitting, to prepare those who were to be baptized in the morning. In the setting of the Easter vigil the mood was one of expectation that the Son of Man would soon return.

Mark a Galilean Gospel

Not all scholars are convinced that Rome is the setting for Mark's Gospel. Several have proposed that the evangelist composed the Gospel in Galilee either before or after the destruction of Jerusalem. Unlike the Roman hypothesis, there is for Galilee no external evidence, such as the patristic testimony which locates Mark at Rome and identifies the author as the interpreter of Peter. Consequently, hypotheses which argue for a Galilean origin must develop their argument on internal grounds, i.e., data from within the Gospel itself.[19]

One such hypothesis is that of Willi Marxsen who contends that Mark wrote in or near Galilee before the destruction of Jerusalem in order to summon the community to Galilee where Jesus' *parousia* (return as the Son of Man) will take place. In *Mark the Evangelist*[20] Marxsen develops this position by studying the manner in which the evangelist writes about the land of Galilee. Galilee, according to Marxsen, is more than a geographical area;

in the Gospel it becomes a place endowed with theological significance.

First, Galilee is the place of Jesus just as the wilderness is the place of John the Baptist. Jesus comes from Galilee, he begins his ministry there, and it is there that he calls his first disciples. From Galilee Jesus' fame spreads throughout the surrounding region, and to Galilee people come to see and hear him. Galilee, according to Marxsen, "is not to be taken strictly as the area west of the Sea, but as including the territory around the Sea."[21] This means that properly speaking there is no mission outside of Galilee in the first part of Mark's Gospel. So one gets the impression that the evangelist wants to describe all of Jesus' activity as taking place in Galilee.

Second, the evangelist's purpose in describing Jesus' activity in Galilee must be read in the light of the Markan community for whom Galilee, and perhaps the Sea of Galilee, has special significance. A clue to this can be found in two related texts, 14:28 ("But after I am raised up, I will go before you to Galilee") and 16:7 ("But go, tell his disciples and Peter that he is going before you to Galilee; there you will see him, as he told you"). Although these texts are usually understood as references to the appearance of the risen Lord to the disciples, Marxsen interprets them in relationship to the *parousia*. Thus the Markan Gospel is a sermon which summons Christians to the land of Galilee where the risen Lord will soon return.

In what setting would such a "Gospel-sermon" be composed? Marxsen points to A.D. 66, the eve of the Jewish war, when the primitive Christian community of Jerusalem supposedly fled to Pella which is on the west side of the Jordan River.[22] The community would have fled not only because of the impending war but because of a heightened sense that the *parousia* was at hand. So the evangelist writes for a community already in Galilee which awaits the *parousia* and another which has journeyed to Galilee with the same hope. Galilee becomes a Christian Holy Land.

Werner Kelber, *The Kingdom in Mark: A New Place and a New Time,*[23] agrees with Marxsen that the setting for the Gospel is Galilee. "Galilee in its broadest sense, including the Decapolis and the area of Tyre and Sidon as outlined by Mark, furnishes the setting in life for Mark the evangelist."[24] Kelber concurs that hope for the *parousia* is a major reason why the Gospel was composed. However, he differs from Marxsen by situating the Gospel in the aftermath of the Jewish war and the destruction of Jerusalem. Furthermore, Kelber argues that the Gospel was written as a polemical work of the north (Galilee) aimed at the ruined tradition of the south (Jerusalem).

According to this reconstruction, Jerusalem Christianity betrayed Jesus' original vision. Self-styled Christian prophets of Jerusalem fell into an eschatological "heresy." During the turbulent years of the Jewish war, these "*parousia* prophets" proclaimed Jerusalem as the site of the kingdom and announced the imminent arrival of the Son of Man who would deliver them from the Romans. Against this background, Kelber interprets the apocalyptic discourse of chapter thirteen.

That chapter tells the Christians of Mark's community that the time of the Jewish war was not the eschatological moment of the Son of Man as the *parousia* prophets falsely foretold. Rather, that period is yet to come, but it will occur in a new place (Galilee, not Jerusalem) and at a new time (after, not before, the Jewish war).

The setting for Mark's Gospel, therefore, is Galilean Christianity in the aftermath of the Jewish war. The established Christianity of Jerusalem, a Christianity less than enthusiastic about Gentile Christians, was led astray by *parousia* prophets and finally destroyed. Mark the evangelist writes to Jewish and Gentile Christians to provide a new synthesis. For this community Galilee is the new Jerusalem as Jesus had designated forty years earlier. In Galilee the community will find its future: the *parousia*. Since Galilee is not bound to city and temple, it becomes an open space where Jew and Gentile can be one as Jesus intended.

Mark a Syrian Gospel

In *Community of the New Age: Studies in Mark's Gospel*,[25] Howard Clark Kee suggests that Mark's community was based in southern Syria (north of Galilee) and that the evangelist writes shortly before the fall of Jerusalem. Since Kee judges that Mark's Gospel manifests an apocalyptic atmosphere, he employs sociological models drawn from other apocalyptic communities to understand the shape and contour of Mark's community. These models lead him to conclude that the evangelist writes for a community which has been influenced in two ways. First, it is an apocalyptic community after the style of the Hasidim and Essene communities which emerged in Judaism about the time of the Maccabean revolt (167–164 B.C.). Second, the community gained new adherents by means of itinerant preachers who went from village to village in the style of the Cynics and Stoics, performing healings and exorcisms.

According to Kee, the Markan community saw its own mission modeled in Jesus' itinerant mission to the Gentile regions of Tyre, Sidon, and the Decapolis. Like Jesus' original disciples, and like Cynic-Stoic itinerant charismatic preachers, members of the Markan community went from village to village preaching, healing, and performing exorcisms (3:14–15; 6:13). Such a career, of course, demanded a break with one's natural family and required a redefinition of family as provided in Mark 3:31–35.

The importance devoted to setting aside ritual laws of clean and unclean (7:1–23) indicates that this community was liberated from the Mosaic law. The Gentile mission played a special role in its preaching, and in Kee's view "the community was open across social, economic, sexual, and ethnic barriers."[26]

As an apocalyptic community, the Markan congregation had its esoteric aspects. It was convinced that God had granted it special revelation by which it could understand the goal and purpose of creation. God had given the mystery to them alone, while everything remained an enigma to outsiders. This is evident in Mark's use of parables in which Jesus employs the parables to prevent outsiders from understanding the mystery of the kingdom (4:11-12). It also appears in the many private instructions Jesus gives to his disciples (9:28; 10:10; 13:3-37).

The use of Aramaic expressions suggests that Mark wrote for an audience which could identify with this Semitic linguistic background. But the author's mistaken notion of Galilean geography speaks against a Galilean origin. Consequently, Kee sees the Markan community based to the north of Galilee in "rural and small-town southern Syria."[27] There the evangelist wrote for a covenant people who fervently believed that God would reward their fidelity in the near future.

Conclusion

Scholars have not reached a consensus as to when and where the Gospel of Mark was composed. Although the question is still open, my preference is for a Roman origin shortly before the destruction of Jerusalem. The external evidence for Rome is strong, although it can be disputed, and there is no similar evidence for Syria or Galilee. Furthermore, although it is not decisive, the internal evidence also suggests a Roman origin.[28] I point to only two indications. First, Mark 10:11-12, Jesus' teaching on divorce, presupposes a setting in which a woman has the right to divorce her husband. Such a right was granted in Roman law but not in Jewish law. This seems to point to a Roman setting. Second, in 12:42, the story of the widow's mite, the evangelist explains that the woman's two copper coins are equivalent to a penny, a *kodrantēs*. Such a coin was not used in the area of Syria and Galilee, but it was used in Rome.[29]

The question of when the Gospel was composed hinges upon one's interpretation of chapter thirteen. Does this chapter presuppose the destruction of Jerusalem and its temple or does it merely suggest that the end is imminent? In my view, there is no decisive evidence that the events have already occurred. Much of the language in the discourse is dependent upon the Book of Daniel and other apocalyptic imagery. If this is so, the author is probably writing during the period of the Jewish war (66–70) with an intuition that the city's destruction is at hand. The destruction, however, has not yet taken place.

Who is this author? More than likely he was a Christian named Mark. The tradition which associates him with John Mark of the Acts of the Apostles, however, is more difficult to substantiate since Mark was one of the most common names in the Roman empire. If this Christian named Mark did indeed write from Rome, it is likely that he had contact with Peter. Thus the importance of his Gospel. But as we shall see in a later chapter, Papias' description of Mark as the interpreter of Peter oversimplifies the manner in which the Gospel was composed and needs refinement.

If the questions of date, place and authorship must remain open, so must the question concerning the community that the evangelist addressed. The Roman hypothesis views the community as stable but under, or about to fall under, persecution. The Galilean hypothesis views the community as eagerly awaiting the imminent *parousia*. The Syrian hypothesis views the community as composed of itinerant preachers who also have a high degree of apocalyptic expectation. Furthermore, the hypotheses of Brandon and Kelber view Mark's Gospel as standing in opposition to the Jewish form of Christianity based in Jerusalem. The position one adopts regarding the place of origin strongly influences one's view of the community and so the Gospel's setting.

Nonetheless, something can be said about Mark's community. First, the evangelist writes to a congregation that is predominantly, but not necessarily exclusively, Gentile Christian. This congregation no longer observes the Mosaic law. Second, the congregation has experienced, or is about to experience, persecution. This persecution, or its threat, has led to an apocalyptic atmo-

sphere within the community. Many of the members of the community believe that the end is imminent and that Jesus, the Son of Man, will soon return. In face of this, Mark writes to quiet excessive apocalyptic expectation. The end is near, but certain things must occur before the Son of Man returns. Finally, the community has forgotten the centrality of the cross in the life of discipleship. Most importantly, then, Mark writes to remind them of the cross and the true meaning of discipleship.

In my view the setting for Mark's Gospel is a predominantly Gentile community, threatened by persecution, excited by apocalyptic speculation, and forgetful of the cross. The Roman community of the late 60s, a recent victim of Nero's persecution and now fearful of the outcome of the Jewish war, is a likely candidate.

2
The Christology of Mark's Gospel

In recent years, Markan students have become keenly aware that the Second Gospel contains a profound Christology centered on the cross. More forcefully than any other evangelist, Mark argues that no one can comprehend the mystery of Jesus' identity apart from his crucifixion and death on the cross. It is significant, therefore, that Mark concludes his story with the account of the empty tomb (16:1–8)[1] and not with an appearance story of the risen Lord. It is the evangelist's way of saying that the risen Lord can only be met by those who follow the way of discipleship marked out by the crucified one during his earthly ministry.

Markan Christology, however, is not a systematic presentation of Jesus' person as is found in the creeds of the Church or manuals of theology. It is an implicit Christology rather than a systematic treatment, and the reader should not expect to find all aspects of Christology within the Gospel, e.g., the eternity and pre-existence of Christ.[2] Nonetheless, Mark's Gospel contains a rich Christology which continues to challenge the Church even today.

In recent scholarship, there have been at least two methodological approaches to this Christology. First, several authors have focused upon the titles which the evangelist attributes to Jesus. When assembled, they form an impressive list.[3] Mark designates Jesus as Christ/Messiah (1:1; 8:29; 14:61; 15:32), Son of God (1:1,11; 3:11; 5:7; 9:7; 14:61; 15:39), Son of Man (2:10,28; 8:31,38; 9:9,12,31; 10:33–34,45; 13:26–27; 14:21,41,62), Rabbi (9:5; 10:51; 11:21; 14:45), Teacher (4:38; 5:35; 9:17,38; 10:17, 20,35; 12:14,19,32; 13:1; 14:14), King (15:2,9,12,18,26,32), Holy One of God (1:24), Bridegroom (2:19), Prophet (6:4,15; 8:28), Son of David (10:47–48), the Coming One (11:9), Shepherd (14:27), and the Mightier One (1:7). Scholars who concentrate upon the titles applied to Jesus try to determine if there is a hierarchy within this list as well as the precise meaning of each title. For example, does Mark understand Jesus primarily as the Son of Man or as the Son of God? How do these and other titles such as Messiah relate to each other? How did the evangelist interpret these titles? Did he conceive of Jesus as the royal, Davidic Son of God or as a Hellenistic Son of God, a "divine man"?

While nearly all would agree that the titles Mark applies to Jesus are important, many would contend that his Christology involves more than the examination of these titles. Consequently, a second methodological approach focuses upon the person of Jesus as presented in Mark's narrative or story.[4] These scholars point out that "the discussion and explanation of christological titles is not basically Mark's way of doing christology."[5] Rather, "Mark's narrative is already a christology,"[6] inasmuch as the Gospel presents a portrait of Jesus. Robert Tannehill writes:

> Jesus is the central figure in the Gospel of Mark, and the author is centrally concerned to present (or re-present) Jesus to his readers so that his significance for their lives becomes clear. He does this in the form of a story. Since this is the case, we need to take seriously the narrative form of Mark in discussing this Gospel's presentation of Jesus Christ. In other words, we need ways of understanding and appreciating Mark as narrative Christology.[7]

While we have spoken of two methodological approaches—examination of titles and study of Mark's narrative—most scholars in fact employ elements from both. Those studying titles must ask how they function within Mark's story, and those investigating narrative must inquire what titles the author uses and how he handles them.

Today, students of Mark's Christology continue to debate what the significance of his story is for his Christology and why he employed the titles he did. Was Mark developing a traditional Christology which he received from the tradition? Was he combating a false Christology which threatened his community? Central to these questions and to Mark's Christology is the so-called "messianic secret" popularized by Wilhelm Wrede at the beginning of this century. His book, *The Messianic Secret,*[8] initiated the modern debate surrounding Mark's Christology. Both those who examine Mark's Christology from the point of view of titles and those who study Mark's narrative have found it necessary to deal with the questions Wrede raised. In this chapter, we will begin with an explanation of Wrede's proposal and its consequences for the contemporary debate. Next, we will examine how scholars have responded to Wrede's work. On the one hand, many argue that Mark writes to "correct" a false Christology within his community. In most cases such scholars see the title Son of Man as a corrective of the title Son of God. On the other hand, several exegetes view Mark's Christology in terms of Son of God and pay greater attention to the narrative flow of Mark's story. They understand the Jesus of Mark's Gospel as the royal Son of God or as God's faithful servant. We will survey both approaches.

The Messianic Secret

Messianic secret is a technical term in Markan scholarship first introduced by Wilhelm Wrede.[9] Writing at the turn of the century, when scholars were primarily concerned with the quest for the historical Jesus, Wrede argued that the Gospel of Mark was a theological statement of Jesus' identity rather than an objective account of his life. The core of Wrede's argument was his contention that during Jesus' public ministry he neither identified himself as the Messiah nor was he recognized as such. In Wrede's view, it was only after the resurrection that Jesus was acknowledged as the Messiah. In brief, Wrede's agenda was to demonstrate that, contrary to conventional wisdom, the Gospel of Mark was not a reliable foundation upon which to build a life of Jesus; it presented Jesus' life as messianic when in fact it was not.

In order to support his thesis, Wrede pointed to the secrecy motif found in Mark's Gospel. This consists of Jesus' commands silencing demons (1:25,34; 3:12), people whom he healed (1:43–45; 5:43; 7:36; 8:26), and the disciples (8:30; 9:9) not to disclose his messianic dignity. In addition to these, Wrede noted Mark's parable theory (4:10–13) that the mystery of the kingdom was reserved for insiders, and several misunderstandings on the part of the disciples (4:13,40–41; 6:50–52; 7:18; 8:16–21; 9:5–6,19; 10:24; 14:37–41) who, despite the special instruction they received from Jesus, continued to be ignorant of his true identity. Wrede argued that this secrecy motif did not derive from the historical Jesus but from the early Church, and that it was developed by Mark to explain why Jesus was not recognized as the Messiah during his earthly life. In a word, Jesus kept his messiahship a secret by forbidding people to reveal his messianic identity.

Wrede viewed the messianic secret as a transitional concept that arose after Jesus' resurrection when the Church realized that he was the Messiah. Acknowledging Jesus' messiahship, the Church concluded that there must have been some evidence of this during Jesus' earthly life. However, since no one could remember such evidence, the Church concluded that Jesus kept his messiahship a secret until after his resurrection.[10] It was this messianic secret that Mark developed in his Gospel.

Although few scholars subscribe to Wrede's thesis without

qualification, most would agree that he identified an important, if not a key, element of Mark's Christology. In Mark's Gospel, Jesus' identity is not immediately apparent to the human characters within the story. Only the demons know that Jesus is the Son of God since they are supernatural beings, but Jesus silences them. What is the reason for this secrecy? Does the motif derive from the tradition which Mark inherited, and did the evangelist merely appropriate it? Or is the secrecy motif Mark's literary invention and the key to his Gospel? How one answers such questions determines one's view of Mark's Christology.

Ulrich Luz in an important essay entitled "The Secrecy Motif and the Marcan Christology"[11] made an important contribution to the discussion when he separated the commands to silence associated with Jesus' miracles from the commands to silence addressed to the demons and those, after Caesarea Philippi (8:27–30), directed to the disciples. Strictly speaking, the commands associated with the healing miracles are not part of the messianic secret. Their constant violation by those healed shows that miracles cannot remain secret, even when Jesus does not want them to be made known.[12] In other words, despite Jesus' commands, the proclamation of his deeds spreads abroad. Thus these commands further the publication of Jesus' power rather than conceal it. His power is so great that it cannot be hidden.

For Luz, the true messianic secret is found in those commands to silence which concern Jesus' identity. The messianic secret is

> Jesus' messiahship, or as Mark would say in his own terms, Jesus' divine sonship, which remains hidden from the world and is known only to the demons—due to their supernatural knowledge—and since Caesarea Philippi to the disciples—through the miracle of Jesus' authority which they repeatedly experienced.[13]

Heikki Räisänen[14] applauds the manner in which Luz separates the commands to silence which are associated with the miracles from those addressed to demons and the disciples. The real secrecy motif is only found in the latter set of commands. "The secret concerns Jesus' nature or identity: the fact that he is the 'Son of God' or the 'Christ' must be kept secret."[15] Räisänen attributes this real messianic secret to Mark and surmises that, for the evangelist, there was something important about Jesus' identity which can only be recognized after his death. However, Räisänen is convinced that Mark is building upon earlier tradition and was not completely consistent in his presentation. So he cautions, "Whoever claims to know precisely what Mark was aiming at with his secrecy theory is probably over-reaching himself."[16]

In sum, today most scholars agree that the secrecy theme plays an important role in Mark's Christology. To this extent Markan scholarship is in Wrede's debt. Moreover, most concur that the secrecy concerns Jesus' identity which cannot be understood apart from the cross. However, scholars have yet to discover the reason why Mark, or his tradition, introduced this motif and precisely how it functions. In what follows we shall examine some of the solutions which have been proposed.

Corrective Christology

In recent years the American discussion of Mark's Christology has focused upon the supposed intention of the evangelist to "correct" a false Christology threatening his community.[17] Although scholars suggest different scenarios for this alleged Christological "heresy," many would agree with the following general description.

Certain members of Mark's community viewed Jesus as a *theios aner*—that is, a "divine man" infused with the power of the Spirit.[18] As a divine man, Jesus enjoyed miraculous powers and extraordinary wisdom and was acclaimed as the Son of God. Proponents of this divine man Christology emphasized the miraculous and powerful aspect of Jesus' ministry while minimizing and even neglecting his humiliating death upon the cross. For them the stress was upon the present aspect of salvation found in Jesus, the Son of God, the divine man, the bringer of salvation here and now. In a word, theirs was a theology of glory which highlighted Jesus' miraculous power and wisdom while neglecting his suffering and death.

Mark the evangelist, it is asserted, agreed that Jesus was the Son of God. Indeed, the centurion's confession "Truly, this man was the Son of God!" (15:39) is the climactic moment of the Gospel. However, Mark understood the content of this title in a way different from his opponents. For him the most important dimension of Jesus' life was not his miraculous power or divine wisdom but his saving death upon the cross. Consequently, in order to give the Son of God title its proper interpretation, the evangelist juxtaposed it with a second title, Son of Man, which emphasized Jesus' suffering and death (8:31; 9:31; 10:33–34) as well as his future exaltation (8:38; 13:26; 14:62). In sum, Mark countered the divine man Christology with a theology of the cross centered upon the suffering Son of Man. He did not merely reject the Christology of his opponents, he corrected it by demonstrating that the authentic meaning of Son of God resides in an understanding of Jesus as the suffering Son of Man. Thus the proponents of this approach understand Mark as one who corrects the false Christology of his adversaries.[19]

The view of Mark's Christology as corrective provides a coherent response to the questions raised by Wrede more than eighty years ago. The so-called messianic secret is Mark's invention— his way of demonstrating that nobody can understand who Jesus is until he is revealed as the suffering Son of Man. Thus Mark conceals Jesus' identity as the Son of God until the reader fully comprehends the mystery of the suffering Son of Man.

This exposition of Mark's Christology as corrective has been undertaken by many commentators, but in this country the seminal work was Theodor Weeden's *Mark: Traditions in Conflict.*[20] This book influenced many scholars, especially the late Norman Perrin and several of his students.

According to Weeden, Mark's Gospel contains a conflict manifested in the Christological positions espoused by the two main characters of his story: Jesus and the disciples. In this conflict, the disciples adamantly hold to a *theios aner* Christology while Jesus represents a suffering servant Christology. According to the *theios aner* Christology of the disciples:

> Jesus is characterized as the epiphany of God, the divine savior in human form, who intervenes in human affairs to work miracles in behalf of man. He is not a deity, but superhuman—a combination of divine and human. He is imbued with the power and authority of God, and possesses supernatural knowledge and wisdom which he selectively reveals as divine revelation to those of his own choosing.[21]

By contrast, Mark's own Christology, found in Jesus' understanding of himself, "underscores the suffering-servant role of Jesus in the passion predictions and other allusions Jesus makes to his suffering and death (8:31; 10:38–39,45; 12:7–8; 14:8,24, 27,34ff.)."[22]

At this point, one must keep in mind that Weeden is not talking about the historical Jesus and his disciples but about the Jesus and the disciples who are characters within Mark's narrative. These characters represent two distinct Christological positions within the Markan community: the evangelist's own stance reflected in the self-understanding of Jesus, and the opponents' view portrayed in the Christology of the Markan disciples. Mark's community was infiltrated by this second, heretical Christology because certain divine men (*theioi andres*) obtained a hearing within his church. They spoke of Jesus as a great miracle worker and of themselves as recipients of secret teaching about God and Jesus.[23] To combat them and their theology, Mark writes a Gospel in which the disciples of Jesus represent this heretical stance. Because of their obduracy, according to Weeden, the disciples of Mark's story never receive the resurrection message since the fearful women do not report the angel's message to them (16:6–8). Thus Mark suggests that the *theioi andres,* represented by the disciples, never received the full Gospel message; their understanding of the Gospel is defective. So Mark's Gospel is a clever assault on a false Christology. "He takes his opponents' christological title, *Son of God,* empties it of its *theios-aner* connotation, and associates it with the suffering Son-of-man christology, thereby turning it into a title appropriate for his own theology."[24]

If we return to the question of the messianic secret, we see that Weeden provides a new interpretation of the data.[25] In his view, the messianic secret as propounded by Wrede (concealment of Jesus' messiahship) is not the key to Mark's Gospel. Rather, the persistent failure of the disciples to understand Jesus' identity is Mark's polemic against those who espouse the divine man Christology represented by the disciples in the Gospel story. It is not because of a messianic secret that the disciples cannot grasp who Jesus is but because of their obdurate adherence to a false Christology which views Jesus' divine sonship in terms of his being a divine man.

Not all authors have reconstructed the supposed false Christology which afflicted Mark's community in such detail. Norman Perrin approved of Weeden's work but seemed less inclined to speculate about the circumstances surrounding the "heresy" which threatened Mark's community. Perrin produced several stimulating studies which suggested that Mark creatively employed the Son of Man title to correct and interpret Son of God.[26] Like Weeden, he was convinced that Mark was "concerned with correcting a false Christology prevalent in his church."[27] In his view, Peter's confession at Caesarea Philippi exhibits this false Christology, for immediately after confessing that Jesus is the Messiah, Peter rebukes Jesus for speaking of suffering, rejection, and death (8:32).

Peter: You are the *Christ*.

Jesus: And he began to teach them that the *Son of Man* must suffer many things, and be rejected by the elders and the chief priests and the scribes, and be killed, and after three days rise again.

Peter: And Peter took him and began to *rebuke* him.

Jesus: But turning and seeing his disciples, he *rebuked* Peter, and said, "Get behind me, Satan! For you are not on the side of God, but of men."

In Perrin's view, Mark's Christology is expressed in the Son of Man title which Jesus employs to correct Peter's confession that Jesus is the Messiah. So he writes, "Mark uses Son of Man to correct and give content to a christological confession of Jesus as the Christ."[28]

In order to make his point, Perrin examines the way in which the evangelist makes use of the titles Son of God, Christ, and Son of Man. He notes that neither Christ nor Son of God is especially frequent in Mark. Christ occurs six times (1:1; 8:29; 9:41; 12:35; 14:61; 15:32), but it is used in a titular sense only four times (1:1; 8:29; 14:62; 15:32). Son of God occurs eight times (1:1; 1:11; 1:24; 3:11; 5:7; 9:7; 14:61; 15:39).[29] By far, the most frequent title in Mark is Son of Man which occurs fourteen times (2:10; 2:28; 8:31; 8:38; 9:9; 9:12; 9:31; 10:33; 10:45; 13:26; 14:21[twice]; 14:41; 14:62). Furthermore, Jesus is the only one to use this title, thus granting it special significance as his chosen self-description.[30]

Nonetheless, Perrin recognizes that Christ and Son of God come at key moments with Mark's narrative. At the beginning of the Gospel (1:1), Jesus is identified as Christ and Son of God. At the baptism and transfiguration, God calls Jesus his beloved Son (1:11; 9:7). Peter confesses that Jesus is the Christ (8:29); Jesus is mocked as the Christ (15:32); the high priest asks Jesus if he is the Christ the Son of the Blessed (14:61); the centurion confesses that Jesus was truly the Son of God (15:39). However Perrin argues that Mark "uses 'Christ' and 'Son of God' to establish rapport with his readers and then deliberately reinterprets and gives conceptual content to these titles by a use of 'Son of Man.' "[31]

Thus the cries of the demons (3:11; 5:7) that Jesus is the Son of God should be interpreted by Jesus' designation of himself as the Son of Man who teaches with authority (2:10,28). Again the references to Jesus as Christ (8:29) and Son of God (9:7) in the central portion of the Gospel (8:27–10:45) should be seen in terms of the Son of Man who must suffer and die (8:31; 9:31; 10:33,45). In a similar fashion, the Christology of the final portion of the Gospel must be read in light of Jesus' declarations that the Son of Man must be delivered up to suffering and death (14:21,41). According to Perrin, only in 14:62 (Jesus' confession before the high priest) does Jesus disclose his identity, and here the three titles converge.

| High Priest: | Are you the *Christ,* the *Son of the Blessed?* [Son of God] |
| Jesus: | I am; and you will see the *Son of Man* seated at the right hand of Power, and coming with the clouds of heaven. |

Here, Perrin avers, Mark makes his final correction of Christ and Son of God by the Son of Man title. Because of this, and the previous interpretations of Christ and Son of God in light of Son of Man, Mark can allow the centurion to confess that Jesus was truly the Son of God (15:39) without any further correction. The reader has finally learned to understand that Jesus is the Son of God insofar as he is the suffering Son of Man.

If we return to the messianic secret, we discover that Perrin understands it in light of Mark's Son of Man theology.

> The Messianic Secret is a literary device of the Evangelist, designed to emphasize the importance of a correct understanding of christological confession and christological testimony—the confession and testimony are to be kept secret until they can be properly understood—and to create the narrative opportunity for the teaching of that correct understanding.[32]

Like Weeden, Perrin views Mark as correcting a false Christology which views Jesus the Son of God in terms of a *theios aner*. But the Son of God title can only be acceptable to Mark when it is understood in terms of the suffering Son of Man.

Son of God Christology

In recent years there has been a reaction to the corrective Christology described above.[33] Several authors have challenged the assumption that the idea of a divine man (*theios aner*) was a fixed concept in the Hellenistic world, later adopted by the New Testament.[34] Still others argue that although Son of Man plays an important role in the Gospel, Mark's preferred title for Jesus is Son of God. Moreover, they maintain that the evangelist does not use the Son of Man title to correct or give content to Son of God. Indeed, it is suggested that Mark employs the Son of God traditions to interpret the Son of Man title.[35] Still others contend that the proper understanding of Son of God in Mark should be seen in terms of royal messianism; that is, Son of God indicates that Jesus is the royal, Davidic Messiah.[36]

In an article entitled "The Concept of the So-Called 'Divine Man' in Mark's Christology," Otto Betz raises the question "whether there really existed the concept of such a Divine Man, whether one can speak of him as a generally known 'type' composed of distinguishable features."[37] Answering the question negatively, Betz suggests that there is not "such a complicated Christology in Mark, resulting from two opposing views and a rejected heresy. Mark's main task was to prove that Jesus was indeed the Messiah despite his crucifixion."[38] In a more detailed study, Carl Holladay arrived at similar conclusions. His investigation of texts from Josephus, Philo, and Artapanus convinced him that *theios aner* should not be used as a technical term or a well defined category,[39] and he questioned its usefulness in Christological discussions of the New Testament.[40] Furthermore, he urged that "the time now seems ripe to seek for answers to the two-pronged question of Jesus' divine sonship and his miracles along lines other than *Hellenistic Sitze im Leben* or in terms of a process of Hellenization."[41] This is precisely what several authors have done.

In a study entitled *Jesus, the Son of God*, Carl R. Kazmierski claims that Mark was essentially a conservative redactor who used the Son of God traditions he received to preach the Gospel to the Church. This means that the evangelist did not find anything objectionable in the title Son of God. To the contrary, "the Son of God theology of the gospel of Mark rests firmly on the foundations of the traditions which the evangelist has used."[42] Thus Kazmierski does not view Peter's confession at Caesarea Philippi (that Jesus is the Messiah) as false. To be sure, Peter and the rest of the disciples do not fully understand who Jesus is, but they have taken a great step forward.

But in what sense is Jesus the Son of God? To answer this question, Kazmierski examines several traditions concerning Jesus the Son of God (1:1; 1:9–11; 3:7–12; 9:2–8; 12:1–12; 13:32; 14:32–42; 14:61–62; 15:39). While all of these traditions are crucial to Mark's understanding of Jesus' sonship, Kazmierski finds the focal point in the baptismal scene when God declares to Jesus, "Thou art my beloved Son; with thee I am well pleased" (1:11).

Here most commentators agree that Mark alludes to one or more of the following texts from the Old Testament.

Gen 22:1:   Take your son, your only son Isaac, whom you love, and go to the land of Moriah, and offer him there as a burnt offering upon one of the mountains of which I shall tell you.
[God instructs Abraham to sacrifice his son Isaac]

Ps 2:7:   He said to me, "You are my son, today I have begotten you."
[God addresses his anointed, the Israelite king on the day of the king's coronation.]

Isa 42:1:   Behold my servant, whom I uphold, my chosen, in whom my soul delights, I have put my Spirit upon him, he will bring forth justice to the nations.
[God addresses his chosen servant, either an individual or the nation of Israel.]

Since it is God who identifies Jesus at the beginning of the Gospel, the choice one makes at this point is critical. If the evangelist primarily intends an allusion to Genesis 22, Jesus' person could be interpreted in light of Isaac's willingness to be sacrificed. If Mark mainly intends an allusion to Psalm 2, then a royal Christology that views Jesus as the messianic King is appropriate. And if the evangelist is chiefly alluding to Isaiah 42, then a servant Christology, one which understands Jesus as God's chosen servant, is in order.

Kazmierski's analysis leads him to the conclusion that Mark understands Son of God in terms of Isaiah 42 and Genesis 22, with the clearest parallel being the text from Genesis. Thus Mark sees Jesus as God's faithful servant (Isaiah 42) whose mission is already linked with his death (Genesis 22).[43]

To be sure, this baptismal proclamation of Jesus' identity does not dispel the Markan secrecy motif since God only addresses Jesus (and the reader). It is only through the course of Jesus' life, as he responds in obedience to the Father, that we understand who he is. And, of course, the climax of this disclosure comes with the centurion's confession, "Certainly, this man was the Son of God" (15:39). Thus Mark assures the Church that the glorious sonship of Jesus which it preaches is one with the sonship of Jesus manifested during his earthly life. Mark tells the Church that the Son of God which it confesses was always the Son of God, but to comprehend Jesus as God's Son it is necessary to view the various stages within God's plan as it unfolds in the life of the earthly Jesus. Thus Kazmierski presents a strikingly different portrait of Mark's Christology from that found in the corrective Christologies. Mark is not correcting or substantially altering the traditions of Jesus the Son of God. To the contrary, he employs the Church's traditions of Jesus the Son of God in a positive way to preach to the Church.

Several authors would agree with Kazmierski that the Son of God is Mark's preferred title for Jesus and that the evangelist sees no need to correct this title with Son of Man. Like Kazmierski, they are not convinced that Mark had to combat a *theios aner* Christology. However, they would differ from him inasmuch as they interpret the Son of Man title in terms of royal Christology rather than servant Christology or a Christology based on Genesis 22. Thus they argue that by Son of God Mark intends the long awaited, Davidic King, the royal Messiah. To be sure, the evangelist introduces a new element since he presents the royal Messiah as a crucified Messiah; nonetheless it is a royal Christology. Important representatives of this position are Donald Juel, Hans-Jorg Steichele, and Jack Dean Kingsbury. I have also defended a similar position in *The Kingship of Jesus.* [44]

In a work entitled *Der leidende Sohn Gottes* (The Suffering Son of God), Hans Steichele focuses upon the scenes of Jesus' baptism, the transfiguration, and the centurion's confession to develop the thesis that Mark presents Jesus in terms of royal Christology. In his view, the baptismal scene should be interpreted primarily in terms of Psalm 2, thus identifying Jesus as the messianic King. At the transfiguration God makes a similar declaration (9:7) to Peter, James, and John. Revealed in heavenly splendor, Jesus stands with two heavenly inhabitants, Moses and Elijah. Although there is not as clear a reference to Psalm 2 in the transfiguration scene, the similarity of the declaration here with that of the baptismal scene pulls it into the orbit of royal messianism.

1:11:   Thou art my beloved Son; with thee I am well pleased.
9:7:   This is my beloved Son; listen to him.

The final phrase, "listen to him," should be interpreted in terms of what Jesus has just told his disciples and what he will tell them: as the Messiah he must suffer and die (8:31–38; 9:12,31; 10:33–34).

At the crucifixion, Jesus is confessed as the Son of God for the first time. Steichele argues that an earlier version of the passion narrative, much of which can be found in 15:20b–41, made use of Psalm 22 in order to portray Jesus as a righteous sufferer who died as the messianic King (15:26,32). Steichele believes that Mark developed this narrative further by adding, in part, the centurion's confession. Thus it was Mark who identified the righteous sufferer who died as the messianic King with the Son of God. The evangelist states that in his suffering Jesus is the messianic King, the Son of God.

For Steichele the three declarations of Jesus' sonship (1:11; 9:7; 15:39) must be viewed together. God's declarations at the baptism and transfiguration help to interpret the centurion's confession, just as the centurion's confession aids in understanding them. The one whom the centurion confesses as the Son of God is the messianic King revealed at the baptism and transfiguration. The Son of God whom God reveals at the baptism and transfiguration is the suffering Son of God who dies upon the cross. Thus Steichele finds the key to interpreting Son of God in the Old Testament, especially Psalms 2 and 22. Jesus the royal Messiah (Psalm 2) is the suffering Son of God (Psalm 22).

The primary concern of Donald Juel's *Messiah and Temple* is the trial of Jesus in Mark's Gospel. However, in studying Jesus' confession before the high priest (14:61–62), Juel makes an important contribution to the understanding of Mark's Christology.[45]

High Priest:	Are you the Christ, the Son of the Blessed? [Son of God]
Jesus:	I am; and you will see the Son of Man seated at the right hand of the Power, and coming with the clouds of heaven.

Juel notes that Mark draws a parallel between Messiah and Son of the Blessed (Son of God) in 14:61. In doing so, the evangelist shows that he uses Son of God as a royal title. That is, he understands Son of God as a royal, messianic title equivalent to Messiah. As further confirmation of this, Juel points to the royal imagery which pervades chapter 15 where Jesus is called King six times (15:2,9,12,18,26,32). Especially important is 15:32 where Jesus is mocked as the messianic King: "Let the Christ [Messiah], the King of Israel, come down now from the cross, that we may see and believe." The royal imagery, as well as the high priest's question, shows that Jesus is being condemned as the royal Messiah.

Earlier we noted that Perrin and others employed this text as well as that of Peter's confession at Caesarea Philippi as examples of Mark's corrective Christology: the evangelist corrects Messiah and Son of God by Son of Man. At this point, Juel disagrees. According to him, "The Son of Man saying points to the final vindication of the 'gospel of Jesus Christ, the Son of God.' "[46] In other words, the title is not used to correct Messiah or Son of God but to proclaim that God will vindicate Jesus precisely as Messiah and Son of God. The primary Christological confession of Mark's Gospel, therefore, is Son of God, and this confession should be understood in terms of royal messianism.

While the studies of Kazmierski, Steichele, and Juel deal with important aspects of Mark's Christology, that of J. D. Kingsbury, *The Christology of Mark's Gospel,* provides a comprehensive synthesis. Employing the tools of literary criticism, Kingsbury argues that the baptismal scene (1:9–11) is crucial for Mark's Christology since it provides the reader with God's "evaluative point of view" regarding Jesus' identity. That is, at Jesus' baptism, God declares who Jesus is: his beloved Son. Consequently, from this point forward Mark summons the reader to align himself or herself with God's evaluation of who Jesus is. Jesus is God's unique Son, the Davidic Messiah, the royal Son of God, chosen for messianic ministry. This identity, however, is hidden from the human characters within Mark's narrative.

In the second part of his story, Mark establishes "a 'contrapuntal pattern' according to which demonic shouts that Jesus is the Son of God alternate with questions human characters pose about who Jesus could conceivably be."[47] Thus the demons, as supernatural beings, know that Jesus is the Son of God (1:24; 3:11; 5:7), but human beings are puzzled about Jesus' identity (1:27; 2:7; 4:41; 6:3).

In the final part of his story (8:27–16:8), Mark makes a progressive disclosure of Jesus' identity in three stages.[48] Jesus is the Messiah (8:29), the Son of David (10:47–48), and the Son of God (15:39). The first two of these confessions are correct, but they are also insufficient. When Peter confesses that Jesus is the Messiah, he still does not understand that Jesus must suffer and die as the Messiah. And when Bartimaeus acclaims Jesus as the Son of David, he does not know that as the Son of God Jesus is also David's Lord (12:35–37). Thus, Jesus is more than the Messiah, the Son of David; he is the Son of God.

Only the centurion (15:39) makes a fully adequate confession of Jesus' identity when he proclaims that Jesus was truly the Son of God. His confession is more than the declaration of a converted man; from the standpoint of Mark's narrative, it is the perfect acknowledgement of Jesus' identity. The centurion is the first, and the only human character within the story, to confess that Jesus is the Son of God; and this he does because he sees the way that Jesus died. For Kingsbury, the messianic secret is a misnomer. "The secret of Jesus' identity in Mark is not, characteristically, a 'messianic' secret but the secret that Jesus is the Son of God."[49]

Conclusion

Anyone who has followed the recent discussion of Mark's Christology realizes the important role which Wrede's *The Messianic Secret* continues to play. In a sense, that work has set the agenda for Markan studies in this century. The secrecy motif within the Second Gospel is yet to be explained to the satisfaction of all. It is to the credit of the so-called school of corrective Christology that it has emphasized the importance of Jesus' suffering and death for understanding Jesus' identity. This approach has made a significant contribution to explaining Wrede's messianic secret by showing that no one can comprehend Jesus as the Son of God apart from his suffering and death. Unfortunately this approach is crippled by its investment in the *theios aner* concept and the accompanying hypothetical reconstructions of the "heresy" which Mark combated. Furthermore, in my opinion, it unnecessarily places Son of Man and Son of God in opposition to each other. With the apparent demise of the *theios aner* concept, it appears that this approach has lost its strongest argument.

A more fruitful approach, in my opinion, is that which reads Mark's Gospel as a narrative. Such a method allows the text to speak for itself and is not dependent upon external hypotheses of alleged heresies. Such a reading suggests to me that Mark's preferred designation for Jesus is Son of God and that the so-called messianic secret revolves around this title. The reader of the narrative knows from the start who Jesus is, thanks to the superscription (1:1) and God's declaration at Jesus' baptism (1:11). However, this important information is withheld from the human characters within the narrative until after Jesus' death. Thus the evangelist shows his readers that it is not possible to understand who Jesus is apart from his death upon the cross. No heresy need be posited within the Markan community beyond the "heresy" which afflicts Christians of every age—flight from the cross.

As for the meaning of Son of God, I am convinced by those who view the title in terms of royal Christology. Jesus is the messianic King of David's line. To be sure, Mark understands him as more than a Davidic King. As Messiah King, Jesus is God's beloved Son (1:11; 9:7; 12:5), the one who offers his life as a ransom for many (10:45). Jesus is the one who can call God "Father" with an intimacy reserved to an only son (14:36). Mark's is a high Christology, but it is rooted in Old Testament promises. Jesus is the long awaited, royal Messiah. The paradox which Mark tries to explain to his community is that, contrary to popular expectation, Jesus fulfills his messianic role as the crucified Messiah, the Son of God.

3
The Disciples in Mark's Gospel

A careful reading of Mark's Gospel reveals that, after Jesus, the disciples are the most prominent characters within the narrative. At the beginning of his ministry, Jesus calls Simon, Andrew, James, and John to follow him (1:16–20). From this point on, the disciples are Jesus' constant companions until they abandon him at the moment of his arrest (14:50). But the flight of the disciples, the denial of Peter, and the betrayal of Judas do not end the role of the disciples, for at the close of Mark's narrative, the young man commands the women, "Go, tell his disciples and Peter that he is going before you to Galilee; there you will see him, as he told you" (16:7). From start to finish, therefore, the Gospel of Mark is a story of discipleship.

But the role of the disciples within the Gospel is not without ambiguity. On the one hand, there is an impressive block of material which presents the disciples in a positive light. But on the other side of the ledger, there are several texts which highlight the inability of the disciples to grasp the full meaning of discipleship.

On the positive side, one can point to the generous manner in which the first disciples leave their livelihood in order to follow Jesus (1:16–20), a fact of which Peter later reminds him (10:28). On several occasions, the disciples become the recipients of private instruction so that the secret of the kingdom of God is given to them (4:11). To the disciples, Jesus privately explains the meaning of his parables (4:34) as well as his saying about clean and unclean (7:14–23). From the crowds who follow him, Jesus chooses twelve[1] to be with him (3:13–19). Eventually, he sends the twelve on mission, giving them authority over unclean spirits (6:7–13). When Jesus undertakes his fateful journey to Jerusalem, the disciples accompany him. Three times during the course of that journey (8:31; 9:31; 10:32–34) Jesus predicts his passion and resurrection to the disciples and then gives them extensive teaching on the meaning of discipleship. When in Jerusalem, Jesus gives private instruction to four of the disciples concerning the destruction of the temple and his return as the Son of Man (13:1–37), and the evening before his death, he shares a final meal with them (14:12–31). These texts and others point to a positive portrait of the disciples. Having left all to follow Jesus, they enjoy his company in a unique way and become recipients of special knowledge.

This positive view of discipleship, however, needs to be balanced by a series of other texts which emphasize the obtuseness of these same disciples. Among the most significant are three boat scenes which occur before Peter's confession at Caesarea Philippi and three misunderstandings which happen after each of Jesus' passion predictions. The boat scenes consist of the calming of the storm (4:35–41), Jesus' walking on the water (6:45–51), and Jesus' conversation with the disciples (8:14–21) after the feeding of the four thousand. In each of these scenes, the disciples manifest their inability to understand either Jesus' person or what he has done. Thus after calming the storm, Jesus rebukes them, "Have you no faith?" and they ask, "Who then is this, that even wind and sea obey him?" (4:40–41). After Jesus walks on the sea, the evangelist notes, "and he got into the boat with them and the wind ceased. And they were utterly astounded, for they did not understand about the loaves, but their hearts were hardened" (6:51–52). And in the third boat scene, when Jesus warns the disciples about the leaven of the Pharisees, he complains, "Do you not yet perceive or understand? Are your hearts hardened?" (8:17)

Corresponding to these boat scenes are three misunderstandings after each of Jesus' passion predictions. After the first prediction, Peter rebukes Jesus (8:32). After the second, Mark notes that the disciples "did not understand the saying, and they were afraid to ask him" (9:32). And following this, they argue among themselves about who is the greatest (9:34). Finally, after the third prediction, James and John ask for the seats of honor at Jesus' right and left, and the other ten become jealous (10:35–41). In addition to these examples of incomprehension, we should also recall that the disciples fail. Judas betrays Jesus (14:10–11), the others flee when he is arrested (14:50), and Peter denies him three times (14:66–72). There can be little doubt that although the disciples enjoy a privileged role, they do not completely understand who Jesus is or the full demands of discipleship.

This complex picture of the disciples has resulted in several attempts to explain the data. For Wilhelm Wrede the blindness of the disciples was part of Mark's messianic secret. It was the evangelist's way of showing why Jesus was not recognized as the Messiah during his earthly life. Since Wrede, however, scholars have interpreted the data in other ways. For the sake of simplification, we will categorize their solutions under two headings: the polemical thrust and the paraenetic or pastoral view.[2] According to the paraenetic or pastoral view, the disciples' obtuseness is a literary device employed by the evangelist to instruct his community about the authentic meaning of discipleship. Thus Mark reveres the disciples but uses their failures to instruct his community. His intent in describing the disciples as he does is pastoral; he calls the Church to authentic discipleship.

For other scholars, however, this approach does not sufficiently explain the evangelist's harsh treatment of the disciples. For example, although they are insiders (4:11–12), this situation is reversed in the third boat scene in which the disciples are accused of not understanding, of having hardened hearts, and of not seeing or hearing (8:17–18). Or again, after rebuking Jesus, Peter is called ''Satan'' by Jesus (8:33). Finally, many of these writers argue that the disciples never received the message about the risen Lord since the women at the tomb were afraid and said nothing (16:8). Consequently, some see a polemical thrust in Mark's description of the disciples. They are literary figures who represent a faction of the Church against which the evangelist polemicizes. In most scenarios such as this, Mark is reputed to represent a Galilean, Gentile faction of the Church disputing with a more conservative wing of the Church centered at Jerusalem. The position of this conservative, Jewish wing can be seen in the disciples of Mark's Gospel who do not comprehend the full dimensions of the Christian message.

At this point the reader will recognize a certain similarity with the previous chapter. Once more the investigation of Mark's Gospel is divided between those who interpret it in terms of an external threat afflicting the community and those who see Mark as writing for the community but not necessarily concerned about an external danger. Thus, just as some authors view the Son of God title as being in need of correction by the Son of Man title, so some see the disciples of the Gospel in a negative light. They represent a false position. On the other hand, just as some see the Son of God as a legitimate title, but one which is only understood correctly in the light of Jesus' death, so there are those who view the disciples positively. Mark does not polemicize against them but uses the story of their failure to call Christians to authentic discipleship characterized by a willingness to follow Jesus on the way.

In this chapter we will examine representative views of both positions. Moreover, since Mark's understanding of discipleship serves as an entree to his ecclesiology, we will investigate some of his images for the Church. We will also say something about the twelve who appear to form a smaller group within the larger circle of disciples.

Mark's Polemical Thrust

One of the first attempts to account for the incomprehension of the disciples was a brief essay by Joseph Tyson, "The Blindness of the Disciples in Mark."[3] Whereas Wrede argued that the disciples did not proclaim Jesus' messiahship because they were commanded to remain silent, Tyson contends that they had an incorrect conception of Jesus from the beginning. He writes:

> Mark is not here saying that the disciples understood that Jesus was Messiah and were commanded not to broadcast it; rather he is saying that they completely misunderstood the nature of Jesus' messiahship, not understanding it as a suffering messiahship but as a royal messiahship which would issue in benefits for themselves.[4]

In Tyson's view, Mark's Gospel stands in opposition to the Jerusalem church which was controlled by the members of Jesus' family and some of his original disciples. This church looks upon Jesus as the royal, Davidic Messiah and waits for his return as king. It does not seem interested in the mission to the Gentiles and maintains many Jewish practices. By contrast, Mark's own community represents a Galilean Christianity which focused upon the suffering Son of Man and was intensely concerned for the mission to the Gentiles. For Mark, the death of Jesus was more than an historical event; it had redemptive meaning. Jesus was not a nationalistic Messiah but the Son of Man whose death had significance for the Gentiles. Mark's portrayal of the blindness of the disciples, therefore, must be understood against this historical background. By highlighting the disciples' incomprehension, the evangelist polemicizes against certain of the disciples who have inflated their own importance and have not understood the deepest meaning of Jesus' death. In a word, Mark's Gospel becomes a "window" through which the reader sees a struggle within the early Church.

The work of Etienne Trocmé, *The Formation of the Gospel According to Mark*,[5] is similar to Tyson's essay inasmuch as it posits a struggle between Mark's community, receptive to the Gentile mission, and the Jerusalem community, a more conservative church headed by James, the brother of the Lord. Trocmé writes:

> he [Mark] was the spokesman of an enterprising movement which, having broken away from the mother church of Jerusalem, had launched out into a large-scale missionary venture among the common people in Palestine and in so doing felt that it was obeying the command of the risen Christ and at the same time following his earthly example.[6]

However, whereas Tyson sees the basic issue in the dispute as Christological (royal, Davidic Messiah vs. Son of Man), Trocmé identifies the point of concern as ecclesiological. The leadership of the Jerusalem church has forgotten the real ecclesiological intention of its master. Jesus never set out to establish a dynastic structure within the Church by which members of his family could inherit his office. Thus Mark endeavors to place the leadership of the Church under the rule of the risen Lord. He calls his community to missionary activity modeled upon the itinerant ministry of Jesus. At different points within his story, moreover, the evangelist criticizes well-known Church figures such as Peter, John, James, Andrew, and the members of Jesus' own family. Mark wishes to show that there is no need to have belonged to the small group of Jesus' original followers in order to be a disciple. All that is required "is to have the will to become an itinerant missionary in the service of the Good News and, to that end, to sacrifice fortune, family, and life itself."[7]

According to Trocmé, the Gospel can be outlined in light of Mark's ecclesiological intent. In the first section (1:1–3:12), Jesus calls disciples and people to separate themselves from the old leadership of Israel. The second section (3:13–6:13) deals with the privileges Jesus confers upon the twelve, his new family. A third section (6:14–8:29) deals with the shepherd role which the disciples must now play vis-à-vis the crowds. In the fourth section (8:22–10:52) Jesus provides an apprenticeship in faith and service to prepare the disciples for mission. And in the last (11:1–13:37) he offers his disciples the prospect of sharing in his victory over the wicked leaders of Israel.[8]

Although Trocmé provides an ecclesiological rather than a Christological accent, he stands in the same camp with Tyson. The Gospel serves as a window through which to view a conflict within the Church. Mark depicts the disciples as he does in order to polemicize against the leadership of the Jerusalem church.

In *Mark's Story of Jesus*,[9] Werner H. Kelber espouses a position similar to that defended by Tyson and Trocmé: Mark polemicizes against the disciples and the Jerusalem church. However, Kelber's work differs from theirs in two significant ways. First, in the main chapters of his book, Kelber approaches Mark's narrative as story. Instead of dealing with the question of tradition and redaction, he concerns himself with the narrative flow of the text. This entails setting aside knowledge gained from Matthew, Luke, and John in order to grasp the story line of Mark in all of its originality. For the most part Kelber does not explain the disciples' behavior in terms of the evangelist's historical situation. Rather, he artfully retells the Gospel narrative and contends that "Mark's story is essentially that of the conflict and break between Jesus and the Twelve."[10] In terms of methodology, Kelber makes an advance over his predecessors since he is more attuned to the narrative dimensions of Mark's Gospel.

However, realizing that many readers will be puzzled by the evangelist's relentless criticism of the disciples, Kelber concludes his work with a reconstruction of the historical situation which occasioned the Gospel.[11] Here he establishes a second difference between his work and those mentioned above. Whereas Tyson and

Trocmé identify Christology and ecclesiology, respectively, as the occasion for Mark's polemic against the disciples, Kelber views the reason as eschatological. After the resurrection, the disciples never returned to Galilee as the risen Lord instructed them. Instead they remained at Jerusalem where they mistakenly waited for the arrival of the kingdom and the parousia. Writing after the destruction of Jerusalem and its temple (70 A.D.), Mark attempts to explain the demise of the mother church by showing that forty years earlier (30 A.D.) Jesus announced the arrival of the kingdom in Galilee, not Jerusalem. The catastrophic destruction of Jerusalem, therefore, should not be misunderstood. Jesus always intended that the arrival of the kingdom would be in Galilee. In his narrative, Mark opposes false prophets, the disciples, and Jesus' family because they represent an erroneous eschatological hope nurtured in the Jerusalem church. However, since this historical reconstruction is not the main thrust of Kelber's work, we must say something of his approach to Mark's story.

According to Kelber, Mark begins his story with an announcement of "The Mystery of the Kingdom" (1:1–4:34). At this point the disciples are portrayed in a positive light; they are privileged insiders. However, in a second section, "The Blindness of the Disciples" (4:35–8:21), they emerge as Jesus' true opponents. Jesus makes six boat trips across the lake alternating between Jewish and Gentile territory. By these trips Mark indicates the unity of Jew and Gentile, a point which the disciples fail to grasp. Because of their hardness of heart, they become outsiders. In a third section, "The Suffering of the Son of Man: (8:22–10:52)," Mark spares no effort to illustrate the persistent and incorrigible failure of the disciples, the Twelve, and the triumvirate."[12] Each time that Jesus explains that he must suffer, the disciples fail to understand. In the fourth section, "The End of the Temple: (11:1–13:37), the disciples manifest their incomprehension in yet another way. They mistake Jesus for the Davidic Messiah and think that the temple of Jerusalem is the place associated with God's kingdom. Finally, in a fifth section, "The Coronation in Humiliation" (14:1–16:8), Jesus dies in godforsakenness as the crucified King while the disciples abandon him. Because the women at the tomb are afraid, they never tell the disciples the message of Jesus' resurrection. The disciples mistakenly remain in Jerusalem instead of returning to Galilee.

The common elements in the presentations of Kelber, Trocmé, and Tyson are three. First, they view Mark's community as standing in opposition to the Jerusalem church. Second, they contrast Mark's interest in the Gentile mission with the closed position of the Jerusalem church. Third, they claim that the disciples represent a false theological position, be it Christological, ecclesiological, or eschatological. Consequently, as characters within Mark's Gospel, they are used as opponents of Jesus, and the evangelist's representation of them is polemical.

Mark's Pastoral Intention

Not all commentators are convinced that Mark portrays the disciples as he does for polemical purposes. Most would agree with the judgment of Ernest Best that "his primary objective was pastoral: to build up his readers as Christians and show them what true discipleship is."[13] Best explains that if a writer chooses to speak about discipleship, there are two obvious approaches: portray the disciples as good examples, or instruct the reader through the disciples' failure. Best believes that Mark chose the second approach because (1) Jesus is the hero of the story, (2) the readers of the Gospel knew that the historical disciples failed, (3) discipleship depends on a willingness to accept help from God, and (4) "many of Mark's readers have already failed through public or private persecution or though other causes."[14] Best explains the disciples' failure as part of Mark's pastoral effort to instruct the Church rather than as a polemic against the disciples.

The view that Mark was instructing his community rather than recounting the story of the historical disciples is convincingly elucidated by Karl-Georg Reploh as the title of his work indicates: *Markus—Lehrer der Gemeinde* (Mark—Teacher of the Community).[15] For Reploh the incomprehension of the disciples is an expression of the kind of behavior within the Markan community. Several stories in the first part of the Gospel are intended to remind the community that Jesus himself called and chose the community (1:16–20; 3:13–19; 6:6b–13). Thus the evangelist begins by placing discipleship in a positive light.

However, other stories in the first part of the Gospel highlight the disciples' faulty understanding. Primary among these are Jesus' discussion with the disciples about the leaven of the Pharisees (8:14–21) and Mark's comment in 6:52, "for they did not understand about the loaves, but their hearts were hardened." Other significant texts are 4:13 ("Do you not understand this parable? How then will you understand all the parables?") and 7:18 ("Then are you also without understanding?"). This lack of understanding on the part of the disciples reflects the incomprehension which afflicts Mark's community. For example, the community no longer understands the parable of the sower (4:3–8) or Jesus' saying that "there is nothing outside a man which by going into him can defile him" (7:15). Therefore, Mark must explain these to his community (4:14–20; 7:18–23). Again, the community no longer comprehends the meaning of Jesus' feeding miracles. Therefore, through the Gospel story the evangelist must teach that just as Jesus fed the crowds in the wilderness so he will continue to feed the community even now. What Mark's community lacks and what the Gospel, and in particular the feeding stories, calls for is conversion and faith (1:15).

In the great section on discipleship (8:27–10:52), Mark once more addresses his community. While the passion predictions (8:31; 9:31; 10:33–34) prepare for Jesus' passion and show that the disciples did not understand the way of the cross, Mark's intention goes beyond this. In composing this section, he thinks more of his own community than of Jesus' original disciples. The resistance of the disciples to embracing the way of the cross mirrors the protests and opposition to the same within the evangelist's community. Thus Mark's critique of the disciples' behavior is addressed primarily to his community; it is intended to call the community to the only appropriate conduct: follow Jesus. Like Best, Reploh views Mark as a pastor dealing with difficulties within the Church.

While most exegetes recognize that the disciples' lack of understanding is a major theme in Mark's Gospel, few have examined the specific texts dealing with the theme as carefully as Camille Focant in an article entitled, "L'Incompréhension des Disciples dans le deuxième Évangile" (The Obtuseness of the Disciples in the Second Gospel).[16] After a careful examination of these texts, Focant cautions that we should not be too quick to speak of the disciples' lack of understanding. His analysis reveals that there are two basic types of obtuseness in Mark's Gospel: one positive in nature, the other negative. On the positive side, the disciples often misunderstand Jesus because of the grandeur of a miracle (4:40–41; 5:31; 6:37; 8:4), the harshness of his teaching (8:32–33; 9:32; 10:24,32), or the grandeur of Jesus himself at the moment of an epiphany (9:5–6). Properly speaking, these texts do not belong to the theme of incomprehension. On the other hand, a number of texts do express the motif with a negative judgment upon the disciples (4:13; 6:50–52; 7:18; 8:16–21). According to Focant, these are the texts from which to develop the theme. His analysis convinces him that Mark did not invent the motif; it was already present in the material which the evangelist received from the tradition. Nonetheless, he is the one who systematized it. Why?

Focant's response is similar to Best's and Reploh's inasmuch as he argues that Mark was writing for his community, not polemicizing against the disciples. Mark deals with a fact of history: during Jesus' earthly life the disciples did not completely understand him. But the evangelist's aim was not merely to pursue this historical datum. Mark intends to show his readers how difficult it is to grasp the mystery of Jesus and the cross. An understanding of who Jesus is progresses in stages. Just as Peter confesses Jesus' messiahship but does not know how to integrate the element of suffering, so the reader only understands the mystery of Jesus and the cross in a partial manner. One should not be satisfied too quickly that he or she has pierced the mystery of Jesus and the cross.

These studies share two common traits. First they view Mark as employing the failure of the disciples to instruct his community. Second, their methodological approach is redaction criticism; that is, they endeavor to isolate Mark's editorial activity in order to understand his intent. The approach of Robert C. Tannehill in "The Disciples in Mark: The Function of a Narrative Role"[17] argues that "additions and changes to source material do not in themselves reveal the concerns and emphases of the author."[18] The composition must be examined as a whole. Therefore, employing the tools of literary criticism, Tannehill examines the narrative role which the disciples play in Mark's Gospel. To this extent his article is similar in approach to Kelber's volume. His reading of the narrative, however, leads him to a different conclusion: although Mark criticizes the disciples, he does not reject them. According to Tannehill, Mark's intent is to make the reader identify with the disciples in order to learn from them. Thus, "the more clearly the reader sees the disciples represent himself, the more clearly the necessary rejection of the disciples' behavior becomes a negation of one's past self."[19]

To accomplish this, Mark presents an essentially positive view of the disciples in the first six chapters so that the reader can identify positively with them. The evangelist accomplishes this through three linked scenes: the call of the first disciples (1:16–20), the selection of the twelve (3:13–19), and the mission of the twelve (6:7–13). Thus, although there are suggestions of failure (4:13,40–41), the fundamental presentation of the disciples is positive.

As the narrative develops, however, Mark describes a number of scenes which associate the disciples with Jesus' enemies. Primary among these are the three boat scenes in which misunderstandings occur (4:35–41; 6:45–52; 8:14–21). The last of these is the most crucial. Jesus complains that the disciples do not hear or understand (8:18), a position which identifies them as outsiders (cf. 4:11–12). To underline this, Mark surrounds the scene with two miracles in which Jesus cures deafness and blindness.

7:31–37:   cure of a *deaf* man
8:18:   disciples do not *see* or *hear*
8:22–26:   cure of a *blind* man

In the central portion of the Gospel (8:31–10:45), Mark continues to emphasize the disciples' blindness to Jesus' teaching by a pattern of prediction (8:31; 9:31; 10:33–34), resistance on the part of the disciples (8:32–33; 9:33–34; 10:35–41), and correction on the part of Jesus (8:34–35; 9:33–37; 10:35–45). Thus the reader who originally associated himself or herself with the disciples must review that judgment and ask if his or her stance toward Jesus is also in need of correction.

But what is the evangelist's final judgment of the disciples? Have they been rejected because of their obtuse behavior? It is at this point that Tannehill is most different from Weeden, Trocmé, and Kelber. First, he points to Jesus' apocalyptic discourse (chapter 13) where the Lord warns his disciples that they will also face persecution (13:9–13), and therefore they must not be caught asleep (13:33–37). Inasmuch as Jesus points to the time after his death and resurrection, he establishes continuity between the disciples who have momentarily failed and the future leaders of the Church. If Mark viewed the disciples as enemies, he would hardly have had Jesus predict that they would stand before governors and kings for his sake (13:9).

Second, Tannehill points to Jesus' prediction, "but after I am raised up, I will go before you to Galilee" (14:28). The prediction is recalled by the young man at the empty tomb, "Go, tell his disciples and Peter that he is going before you to Galilee; there you will see him, as he told you" (16:7). Inasmuch as Jesus' predictions are fulfilled throughout the Gospel, the reader can be confident that this prediction will also be fulfilled. The last verse of the Gospel, "and they said nothing to anyone for they were afraid" (16:8), is merely a literary device to remind the reader that even after the resurrection of the Lord, cowardly behavior has not disappeared from the Church.

In a word, the disciples behavior does not forever disqualify them from Jesus' company. He will establish anew his relationship with them. But their behavior does serve as a negative example of discipleship. Henceforth the reader must undergo a self-examination. Like Best, Reploh, and Focant, Tannehill views Mark as a pastor speaking to the Church.

The Twelve

Although we have spoken primarily of the disciples, on several occasions Mark also refers to the twelve. For example, in 3:13–19 Jesus calls and appoints twelve "to be with him, and to be sent out to preach and have authority to cast out demons" (3:14–15). In 4:10–12 the twelve are given the "secret of the kingdom of God." In 6:7–13, Jesus sends them on mission two by two and grants them authority over unclean spirits. In 9:35–50 they receive a long instruction on the requirements of discipleship, and in 10:32–45 Jesus instructs them once more. In Jerusalem they appear to be his special companions (11:11), and they are present at the Last Supper and Jesus' arrest (14:17–50). Finally, it is one of the twelve who betrays Jesus (14:10,20,43).

While some authors have identified the twelve with the disciples,[20] Klemens Stock[21] argues that Mark distinguishes between the two groups. In his view, the twelve are different from the disciples inasmuch as they are sent on mission to perform the work of Jesus in the person of Jesus. Consequently, they should be seen as a core group within the larger circle of disciples.[22] To be sure the disciples, like the twelve, are intimately associated with Jesus, and it is difficult to distinguish between them and the twelve. Nonetheless, the twelve enjoy a unique calling (3:13–19) and work (6:7–13) which sets them apart.

For Stock, the distinctive characteristic of the twelve consists in their relationship to Jesus. They are called to be with him (*mit-Ihm-sein*), and this being-with-Jesus is the foundation of their mission to be messengers of the Gospel. Their relationship with him, however, is not one of partnership or even friendship; he is the sovereign Lord who calls them to be with him. They may reject this relationship, but they cannot establish it. The essence of their call is to be with Jesus, to follow him on the way to Jerusalem, and eventually to suffer the same fate as their Lord. To be sure they are not the only ones with Jesus, but they are the core of those who are. Their flight at the moment of his arrest (14:50) temporarily breaks this relationship, but Jesus promises that he will restore it once he has been raised. After the resurrection the twelve will follow the risen Lord to Galilee, the land where they were with him during the days of his earthly ministry.

For Mark the twelve are not Jesus' adversaries, even though they fail at the moment of the passion. They serve as examples for the Church. The evangelist points to Jesus of Nazareth and the circle of his followers, and he calls his community "back to Jesus." Messengers of the Gospel must stand in a similar, personal relationship of commitment to their Lord.

The Church

At no point in the Gospel does Mark explicitly speak of the Church. In fact, the word ''church'' only occurs three times in the Gospels (Mt 16:18; 18:17 [twice]). Nonetheless, most commentators agree that a study of the disciples and discipleship necessarily results in a deeper knowledge of the Church. In *Following Jesus,* Ernest Best suggests that Mark views the Church through five images: a flock, a temple, a ship, a community of knowledge, and a house and household.[23]

For Mark the Church is the flock once scattered (14:27) but now gathered together by the risen Lord. As Jesus once had compassion upon the crowds ''because they were like sheep without a shepherd'' (6:34), so he now shepherds the Church and feeds it with his word.

For Mark the Church is like a temple. More specifically it is the temple ''not made with hands'' (14:58). On the cross, Jesus is derided as one ''who would destroy the temple and build it in three days'' (15:29). The irony of this mockery is that it is true. Through his death Jesus makes the old temple obsolete and ''through the death and resurrection of Jesus the new community has come into being and Jesus is its centre.''[24]

For Mark the Church is like a ship. During his earthly ministry Jesus used the ship as a pulpit (4:1) from which to preach the word. Within the ship Jesus gives private instruction to his disciples (8:14–21). And when the disciples find themselves in peril upon the sea (4:35–41; 6:46–52), Jesus delivers them and their ship. So the Church continues as a place of instruction for the disciples, and Jesus saves it from trials.

For Mark the Church is a community of knowledge. As Jesus once made a distinction between teaching given to the disciples and that meant for the crowds (4:10–12), so the risen Lord does the same for the Church.

Finally, Mark views the Church as a house and household. John R. Donahue has developed the image of the Church as household and family in his volume, *The Theology and Setting of Discipleship in the Gospel of Mark.*[25] According to Donahue, Mark views the Church as the true family of Jesus (3:20–35), the new family of Jesus (10:29–31), a community of service (10:42–45), and a watchful community (13:33–36). Donahue's investigation leads him to conclude that ''Mark's community seems to be radically egalitarian in nature and the only visible structure of authority seems to be that of mutual service.''[26] For Mark, Church and discipleship are not separable realities. Disciples do not live as isolated individuals but as members of the new community which Jesus has established, the Church.

Conclusion

At this point most readers will recognize that there is an intimate connection between Christology and discipleship in the Gospel of Mark. Both meet at the cross. Just as one cannot understand who Jesus is apart from the cross, so one cannot grasp the true meaning of discipleship unless he or she is willing to follow Jesus ''on the way.'' That way, of course, leads to the cross.

At this point the reader will also note that the different approaches to the disciples in Mark's Gospel bear a strong resemblance to the different approaches to the evangelist's Christology. Just as many scholars see the interpretative key to Mark's Christology in a Christological error which Mark finds it necessary to correct, so many have sought the key for opening Mark's understanding of the disciples in his alleged polemical stance. They contend that he portrays the disciples as he does because he is reacting against the historical disciples and other false leadership groups, groups most likely based in the church of Jerusalem. Thus according to this view, we might speak of Mark's approach to the disciples as one of rejection.

As was the case with Mark's Christology, I do not agree with these attempts to interpret the Gospel by external data which are so hypothetical in nature. In my view, the argument is circular. One develops a working hypothesis from the Gospel, then that hypothesis becomes an external criterion for interpreting the text. Quite frankly we do not know as much about the circumstances surrounding the composition of the Gospel as we would like to know.

I am more convinced by those who view Mark's approach as pastoral. The Gospel instructed the members of Mark's Church much as it instructs us today. Just as we do not always comprehend the full meaning of discipleship, the members of Mark's community found it difficult to follow Jesus ''on the way.'' Mark writes as a pastor calling his community to authentic discipleship. There is no need to posit a polemical thrust.

That Mark portrays the disciples as blind and obtuse does not mean that he views them as adversaries. Ultimately no one can grasp the full dimension of discipleship apart from the cross and resurrection. Within the Gospel story, the disciples have not yet witnessed Jesus' death and resurrection. That they do not completely understand Jesus and the meaning of discipleship is not surprising. Within the context of Mark's story, their blindness is not so much a moral failure as the inevitable outcome of only knowing Jesus apart from his death and resurrection. But even after the resurrection, the disciples never fully comprehend the mystery of Jesus and the cross, as Focant reminds us. The Gospel, with its enigmatic ending, calls the reader again and again to return to Galilee and follow Jesus ''on the way.''

4
The Composition of Mark's Gospel

Introduction

In the first chapter, we noted that Papias, the second century bishop of Hierapolis, described Mark as Peter's interpreter (*hermēneutēs*). While Papias concedes that Mark did not compose his Gospel as an orderly account of Jesus' life he does give the impression that the evangelist's chief source was the apostle Peter.

> Mark, who had been Peter's interpreter, wrote down carefully, but not in order, all that he remembered of the Lord's sayings and doings. . . . Peter used to adapt his teaching to the occasion, without making a systematic arrangement of the Lord's sayings, so that Mark was quite justified in writing down some things just as he remembered them.

On the basis of Papias' account, one might assume that Mark did not employ other sources in addition to Peter's teaching. Thus the composition of Mark's Gospel was thought to be a relatively simple affair. The evangelist composed his work by "interpreting"[1] what Peter said.

This uncomplicated view of the Gospel's composition was relatively uncontested until the rise of the historical critical method in the eighteenth century. With the help of new methodological tools such as source and form criticism, scholars began to question the assumption that Mark's primary source for his Gospel was the oral tradition deriving from Peter.

Investigations of the Gospels of Matthew and Luke revealed that they were dependent upon several sources, written and oral. For example, both Gospels depend upon Mark, a collection of Jesus' sayings, and special material found in the infancy narratives of each Gospel, as well as still other sources. This being the case, it seemed probable that the Gospel of Mark might also be dependent upon a number of sources or pre-Markan traditions, one of which might even be a Petrine source.

In the first part of the twentieth century, the form critics (Bultmann, Dibelius, Schmidt), suggested that the Gospel of Mark derived from a variety of sources such as collections of miracle and controversy stories and an earlier version of the passion narrative. As the form critics studied the Gospel, they became convinced that Mark's primary achievement had been to collect this diverse material and then to connect it by means of appropriate introductions and conclusions. In other words, a variety of sources (pre-Markan material) were available to the evangelist so that his task was to assemble these earlier traditions into a coherent whole.

The manner in which Mark composed his Gospel became and remains an important question since it is considered the earliest of the Gospels we possess. In the view of many authors, Mark's work, despite its abrupt style, manifests an element of genius since it is the beginning of a new genre which we call "Gospel."[2] But if Mark was the first to conceive of a Gospel, what sources were available to him? It does not appear that he wrote without the aid of earlier traditions.[3] Furthermore, how did the evangelist deal with these sources? Did he respect their integrity? Or did he substantially modify and alter them in order to combat their point of view? The question of how Mark dealt with his sources is, of course, dependent upon the first question (which sources were available to him?). Furthermore, since we only have the Gospel of Mark, how can we distinguish the evangelist's sources from his editorial or redactional activity? How can we be sure that what *we* perceive as sources are indeed *Mark's* sources? We must reckon with the probability that he has so rewritten his sources as to make it impossible to identify them.[4]

Because the question of sources is so difficult to answer, there is no unanimity in Markan scholarship regarding the evangelist's sources. As a result, the question of how he employed his sources is also contested. Some argue that Mark was a conservative editor and redactor, the preserver of the tradition, who treated his sources with reverence and did not greatly alter them. Others view him as a skilled literary figure who did not necessarily contradict the tradition but did rewrite it in the way an author might. Finally, others view Mark as a creative theologian who thoroughly altered his sources, even contradicting them in order to make his point. In this chapter we shall investigate some of the theories which deal with the sources available to the evangelist and discuss the views of those who understand Mark either as a skilled literary figure, or as a creative theologian, or as a conservative redactor.

The Sources of Mark's Gospel

Anyone who reads Mark's Gospel with care soon recognizes that the evangelist structured his work so that material of a similar nature is found in clusters or blocks. For example, most of the parables are found in 4:1–34. Nearly all of the miracle stories are in 4:35–8:26, whereas most of the controversy stories occur in 2:1–3:6 and 11:15–12:40. The presence of collections of like stories or sayings has led many to conclude that older collections of material lie behind these clusters. Rudolf Pesch, for example, suggests that the evangelist employed the following pre-Markan traditions:[5]

- A tradition concerning John the Baptist and Jesus (1:2–15).
- A tradition describing a day in Jesus' ministry at Capernaum (1:21a,29–39).
- A collection of stories depicting Jesus in controversy with the religious leaders (2:15–3:6).
- A collection of parables (4:2–10,13–20,26–33).
- A collection of miracle stories (3:7–12; 4:1,35–39,41; 5:1–43; 6:32–56).
- A collection of material for community instruction which was catechetical and exhortatory in nature, dealing with questions of marriage, riches, and rank (10:2–12,17–27,35–45).
- An earlier version of the passion narrative (8:27–33; 9:2–13,30–35; 10:1,32–34,46–52; 11:1–23,27–33; 12:1–12,35–37,41–44; 13:1f; 14:1–16:8).[6]

All of the material listed above represents Pesch's reconstruction of the traditions available to Mark. In order to understand how he arrives at such reconstructions, it will be helpful to examine his view of the Markan miracle collection.

According to Pesch, Mark inherited a collection of miracle stories which presented Jesus as the eschatological prophet who came to save God's people. This collection was originally in the form of a chiasm, i.e., ABCDC'B'A'.

A. Summary (3:7–12). Vast throngs go to Jesus the healer and exorcist.
B. Stilling of the storm (4:35–41). By his power over the wind and sea, Jesus shows himself greater than Jonah; he is like Yahweh.
C. Healing of the Gerasene demoniac (5:1–20). Jesus is the Son of God, the greatest exorcist, the conquerer of heathen disorder.
D. Healing of a woman with a hemorrhage and Jairus' daughter

(5:21–43). Jesus is greater than Elijah and Elisha; he has power over sickness and even death.

C' Feeding of the five thousand (6:32–44). Jesus is the eschatological shepherd of Israel who distributes the fullness of salvation.

B' Walking on the sea (6:45–51). An appearance of Yahweh takes place through Jesus.

A' Summary (6:53–56). Vast throngs come to Jesus the healer who brings salvation.

While several authors would concur that Mark had access to a collection of miracle stories, not all agree about the scope of the miracle collection or its purpose. For example, Paul J. Achtemeier argues for the existence of ''a pre-Markan cycle of miracles, circulating in the form of two catenae, identical in arrangement (sea miracle, three healing miracles, and a feeding miracle) but not in content.''[7]

Catena I	Catena II
Stilling of the Storm (4:35–41)	Jesus Walks on the Sea (6:45–51)
The Gerasene Demoniac (5:1–20)	The Blind Man of Bethsaida (8:22–26)
The Woman with the Hemorrhage (5:25–34)	The Syrophoenician Woman (7:24b–30)
Jairus' Daughter (5:21–23,35–43)	The Deaf-Mute (7:32–37)
Feeding of the Five Thousand (6:34–44,53)	Feeding of the Four Thousand (8:1–10)

In Achtemeier's view, these catenae ''gave expression to a theology which saw in Jesus a glorious *Theios Aner* [a Divine Man] who manifested himself as such by his deeds during his earthly life. . . . "[8] Mark did not concur with this theological portrait of Jesus; nonetheless he incorporated the valuable material found in these catenae and subordinated the portrait of Jesus as a Divine Man to his own Christology of the suffering Son of Man.

The different reconstructions and interpretations of Pesch and Achtemeier are examples of how difficult it has been for scholars to arrive at a consensus about the extent and purpose of the alleged pre-Markan material.

Partly in answer to this difficulty, Heinz-Wolfgang Kuhn undertook a thorough investigation of the older collections which were assumed to be present in Mark's Gospel.[9] At the beginning of his work he lists and evaluates the collections of pre-Markan material which scholars usually suggest. The list is somewhat similar to that given by Pesch:

- a day at Capernaum (1:16–39)
- controversy stories (2:1–3:6)
- a collection of parables (4:1–34)
- a collection of miracles (4:35–5:43)
- two parallel collections of miracle stories, each beginning with a feeding story (6:33–7:37 \ \ 8:1–26)
- a community catechism (9:33–50)
- a community catechism explaining how disciples should behave with regard to children, marriage, and possessions (10:1–31)
- a collection of controversy stories centered in Jerusalem (11:15–12:40)
- an apocalyptic discourse (13:5b–27)

After a discussion of these collections, Kuhn concludes that the most likely candidates for pre-Markan collections are the controversy stories of 2:1–3:6, the parables of 4:1–34, the catechetical material in chapter 10, and the miracle accounts in chapters 4 and 5. Kuhn's analysis leads him to the conclusion that four older collections, developed by Church teachers for the needs of the community, were available to Mark:

- A collection of controversy stories consisting of 2:1–28 which served the practical needs of the community in which there were disputes between Gentile and Jewish Christians regarding the law.
- A collection of parables consisting of 4:3–8,26–29,30–32, intended to console and encourage the Church about the coming kingdom of God.
- A collection of rules for community living consisting of 10:2–12,17–23,25,35–45.
- A collection of miracle stories consisting of 4:35–5:43 (it may also have included 6:34–51) intended for missionaries who presented Jesus as a Divine Man.

Considering the number of pre-Markan collections proposed by other scholars, Kuhn's results seem meager. However, they suggest that Mark did not have as many older collections as previously thought. Indeed, Mark may have been a much more active author than heretofore realized. This is also the view of several American scholars who have challenged three strongly held hypotheses: that Mark had a collection of controversy stories found in 2:1–3:6, that there was a pre-Markan collection of miracle stories, and that there was an earlier version of the passion narrative.

Mark's Literary Skill

Although scholars have not been able to agree about the sources available to Mark, a majority argue that in 2:1–3:6 the evangelist drew upon a collection of controversy stories. The primary reason is the similarity in form and content which characterizes the material of this section; it presents Jesus in conflict with the religious leaders over matters of Jewish law.

2:1–12	The healing of a paralytic and the question of the authority to forgive sins.
2:13–17	The call of Levi and the question of eating with sinners.
2:18–22	A question about fasting.
2:23–28	A question of plucking grain on the sabbath.
3:1–6	A question about healing a man with a withered arm on the sabbath.

To most authors, it appears that Mark has taken over an earlier collection consisting of five controversy stories and inserted it into his Gospel. Even Kuhn, who limits the number of pre-Markan collections to four, is in essential agreement here. Behind 2:1–3:6 there was an earlier collection of controversy stories.

The hypothesis of a pre-Markan collection here, and at other places within the Gospel, suggests that in the composition of the Gospel Mark was a compiler rather than a literary figure; that is, he collected and connected earlier traditions without substantially altering them.

Joanna Dewey[10] has challenged this assumption as well as the hypothesis that 2:1–3:6 represents a pre-Markan controversy collection. Employing the methodology of rhetorical analysis, she argues that even if Mark used a source such as that proposed by Kuhn (2:1–28), he has thoroughly reworked it into a highly sophisticated rhetorical unit.

Rhetorical analysis, Dewey writes, "is the study of the literary techniques and rhetorical structure of a text to see what light such analysis sheds on the interrelationships of the parts of the text and the meaning of the text as a whole."[11] In the case of 2:1–3:6, she argues that the material has been structured concentrically both in its parts and in the whole. In other words, the evangelist employs the rhetorical techniques of chiasm, ring composition and extended concentric structure in order to arrange his material.

What Dewey means is best seen in her analysis of the five

controversy stories; when studied carefully, they reveal the following concentric pattern.[12]

A	2:1–12	The healing of the paralytic
B	2:13–17	The call of Levi/eating with sinners
C	2:18–22	The saying on fasting and on the old and new
B'	2:23–27	Plucking grain on the sabbath
A'	3:1–6	The healing on the sabbath

The first two of these stories (A and B) are concerned with Jesus' relationship to sin and sinners. The last two (B' and A') deal with questions regarding the sabbath. By contrast, the middle story (C) deals neither with sin nor with the sabbath but with fasting. Moreover, while the stories which surround the middle story (B and B') deal with food, the middle story (C) deals with fasting from food. Dewey also notes that the first and last stories (A and A') are healings with the general theme of life vs. death, while the middle stories (BCB') follow the pattern of action, objection, and vindication. Dewey points to many other concentric patterns not only within the five-story complex but within the individual stories themselves.

According to her, this concentric pattern serves as an aid to understanding Mark 2:1–3:6 by bringing separate incidents into a coherent unity. Scholars have long recognized that in terms of linear development the final verse of this section (3:6) is important for the development of Mark's story: "The Pharisees went out, and immediately held counsel with the Herodians against him, how to destroy him." But Dewey suggests that "the effect of the literary unity of the section on the reader is to emphasize that the opponents objected to Jesus' activity as a whole, and to the messianic claim which was the basis of Jesus' actions."[13]

Dewey is aware that one might object that this concentric pattern was already present in the tradition (the alleged pre-Markan controversy collection) and that Mark merely adopted it. Consequently, she searches for other examples of concentric structure within the Gospel in order to establish that concentric structure is a Markan literary technique. Her investigation yields three other examples: the beginning of the Gospel (1:1–8), the chapter of parables (4:1–34), and Jesus' public debates in Jerusalem (12:1–40).

In the case of 4:1–34, she acknowledges that Mark may have been working from an earlier collection of parables, but the present, artistic arrangement of the material in concentric form should be attributed to the evangelist.

A	1–2a	Introduction
B	2b–20	Parable material
C	21–25	Sayings material
B'	26–32	Parable material
A'	33–34	Conclusion

Dewey is not persuaded, however, that Mark built upon an earlier collection of controversy stories in 12:1–40. Rather, "Mark appears to have constructed the section by joining previously independent traditions."[14] Once more, she notices a concentric pattern.

A	1–9	Public teaching:	The parable of the wicked tenants; threat of God's judgment
B	10–12	Public teaching:	Psalm citation; audience reaction
C	13–17	Public debate:	The things of God are to be given to God; audience reaction
D	18–27	Public debate:	The hope in resurrection is real

C′	28–34	Public debate:	The things of God are the commands to love God and neighbor; audience reaction
B′	35–37	Public teaching:	Psalm citation; audience reaction
A′	38–40	Public teaching:	Warning against the scribes; threat of God's judgment

What does Dewey's study reveal about the composition of Mark's Gospel? On the one hand, it recognizes that the evangelist worked with some sources. But a careful rhetorical analysis suggests that he did not haphazardly join individual traditions together like beads on a string. The result of this rhetorical analysis "is the recognition of the ability of Mark as a writer/compiler, the recognition of the extent to which Mark has interwoven the elements of his narrative into a coherent whole."[15]

Robert Fowler[16] has written a study which, like Dewey's, challenges one of the cherished assumptions of Markan scholarship regarding the Gospel's sources. Moreover, like the work of Dewey, his book employs new methodology for reading the Gospel: literary criticism. His basic thesis is that the evangelist created the story of the feeding of the five thousand (6:30–44) on the basis of an older tradition found in the feeding of the four thousand (8:1–10). Furthermore, Fowler argues that Mark is primarily responsible for the order of the material found in chapters 4–8, that section of the Gospel where the majority of the miracle stories are found.

Above, we noted that several authors (Achtemeier, Kuhn, Pesch) contend that Mark had access to a collection of miracle stories which he employed in the composition of chapters 4–8. One of the reasons authors have been persuaded that such a collection existed is the presence of three sets of similar stories within these chapters: two feeding stories (6:30–44; 8:1–10), two sea miracles (4:35–41; 6:45–52), and two similar healing miracles (7:31–37; 8:22–26). Thus a recurring hypothesis is that these miracles, especially the feeding of the five thousand and the feeding of the four thousand, are variants of the same story found in an earlier, pre-Markan cycle of miracles.

Fowler challenges this hypothesis and wonders if Mark was not more actively involved in the composition of this material. Taking up a suggestion made at the beginning of this century by Emil Wendling, Fowler concludes that Mark himself was responsible for one of the feeding stories. However, whereas Wendling thought that Mark composed the feeding of the four thousand on the basis of the feeding of the five thousand, Fowler argues for the opposite position. The absence of Markan vocabulary and Markan literary characteristics in 8:1–10 leads him to conclude that the bulk of Mark 8:1–10 came to the evangelist from the tradition. By contrast, an examination of the language in Mark 6:30–44 convinces Fowler that Mark composed the feeding of the five thousand in its entirety.

Having set forth this relationship, Fowler says that it is the evangelist who created the tensions between the two stories, and that the feeding of the five thousand (Mark's composition) is the backdrop against which the feeding of the four thousand (the traditional story) is to be read. Thus in writing the story of the five thousand, Mark portrays the disciples as acrimonious and obtuse. They wish to send the crowds away, and when Jesus tells them to give the crowds something to eat themselves, they object that they should have to spend their own money (6:36–37). The crux of both feeding stories is the interaction of Jesus with his disciples, and it is only against the backdrop of the feeding of the five thousand that the reader perceives the blindness and denseness of the disciples when they say, in the second feeding story, ''How can one feed these men with bread here in the desert?'' (8:4). Fowler's initial insight, therefore, is that Mark has written with considerable literary skill in the composition and arrangement of the two feeding accounts.

In addition to the two feeding stories, Fowler also points to the two sea miracles (the calming of the storm and Jesus walking upon the sea) and to the two similar healing miracles (the healing of a deaf and dumb man, and the healing of a blind man) found in this section. He does not submit these accounts to the same rigorous analysis by which he investigated the feeding stories; nonetheless he proposes that "Mark is once again manipulating how we perceive one story by stationing a comparable story as a backdrop for it."[17] Thus in the case of the sea stories, we are amazed that the disciples mistake Jesus for a ghost (6:49) despite the fact that Jesus had earlier calmed the storm and saved them (4:35–41). And in the case of the two healing stories, the repetition of two similar stories provides "an indirect commentary on the disciples' lack of perception by exhibiting individuals who *are* able to hear, speak, and see."[18]

In brief, Fowler contends that these double stories and their placement have more to do with Mark's literary skill as an author than with an earlier source. So Fowler writes, "All the facts seem to demand the immediate abandonment of all talk about double, pre-Markan traditions in Mark 4–8."[19] In Fowler's view, the three sets of double stories in Mark 4–8 overlap and form a chainlike structure which should be attributed to the evangelist.

Sea Miracle	Feeding of 5000	Sea Miracle	Healing	Feeding of 4000	Healing
4:35–41	6:30–44	6:45–52	7:31–37	8:1–10	8:22–26

Fowler's work makes two significant contributions to Markan studies. First, as in the case of Dewey's book, it establishes Mark as a literary figure. Even if the evangelist drew from a collection of miracles, his work as an author in chapters 4–8 is substantial. Not only did he arrange the material by connecting it with appropriate introductions and conclusions, he also created material such as the feeding of the five thousand in order to form the appropriate backdrop for reading other material.

Second, as with Dewey's work, Fowler has introduced a new methodology for reading the Gospel: literary criticism. He is more interested in reading the Gospel as a narrative than in separating redaction (Mark's editorial work) from tradition (Mark's source material). In his view, the attempt to read the Gospel primarily in terms of the changes and alterations the evangelist has made upon his source material is mistaken. The Gospel of Mark is a unity, a literary work in which an author speaks to an audience. The more profitable way of reading the Gospel is in terms of literary criticism. Thus, Fowler makes four methodological points regarding his reading of the Gospel.[20] First, he speaks of Mark as an author and not simply as an evangelist or redactor. Second, he views the Gospel as a literary work to be studied as such. Third, his primary concern is the meaning and message of this literary work. Fourth, he finds it more advantageous to speak of the author's readers or audience rather than to refer to an unknown community to which the Gospel was first addressed.

The works of Dewey and Fowler imply that it may be more profitable to concentrate upon the manner in which Mark has arranged his material than upon a search for his sources and the alterations he has made to them.[21] Neither Dewey nor Fowler suggests that redaction and source criticism be abandoned. But their efforts demonstrate the advantage of new methodologies, methodologies whose results imply that Mark was an author of considerable literary skill.

Mark as a Creative Theologian

Until recently there has been a consensus among NT scholars that a relatively fixed form of the passion narrative was one of the traditions which Mark inherited and incorporated into his Gospel.

The view of Martin Dibelius has influenced many: "The relatively fixed character of the Passion narrative in the synoptics, and the quite unique agreement between John and the other evangelists in this part of the narrative, show that this material had duly and uniformly reached its definite form."[22] Consequently, most scholars assumed that while Mark may have substantially altered his other sources and even developed new material in chapters 1–13, the evangelist did not exercise the same redactional activity in chapters 14–16 (the passion narrative). Here, it was argued, he respected the tradition and did not change it in any substantial way. Indeed, it was assumed that some form of the passion narrative (usually called the pre-Markan passion narrative) was among the first pieces of oral tradition put to writing for use in the Church's liturgy and missionary activity.[23]

For some authors, however, the traditional hypothesis of a pre-Markan passion narrative presents a problem inasmuch as the passion is so clearly the climax of Mark's Gospel. Werner Kelber states the difficulty when he writes: "The very evangelist who has such a vested interest in a theology of death as do few early Christian writers is supposed to have refrained from making a single contribution to the narrative dramatization of Jesus' passion."[24] While Kelber states the difficulty in a dramatic fashion (he is arguing against the position of Rudolf Pesch), his point is well taken. If Mark was editorially active in the first part of the Gospel, should we not expect the same redactional activity in what the evangelist presents as the climax of his work?

Several authors, especially Americans, have pursued this line of thought and argued that Mark did not inherit an earlier passion narrative, or, if he did, that he substantially rewrote it in the light of his theological concerns. Many of these authors presented their findings in *The Passion in Mark*.[25] The results of these studies are summarized in three theses.[26]

First, *"virtually all major (and a multiplicty of minor) Mkan themes converge in Mk 14–16."* Thus, themes such as Mark's portrait of Jesus, the temple, and the disciples which are prominent in chapters 1–13 are also present in the passion narrative.

Second, *"Mk 14–16 constitutes a theologically inseparable and homogeneous part of the Gospel whole."* Thus, chapters 14–16 should not be seen as substantially different from the rest of the Gospel since chapters 1–13 dovetail into them.

Third, *"the understanding of Mk 14–16 as a theologically integral part of the Mkan Gospel calls into question the classic form critical thesis concerning an independent and coherent Passion Narrative prior to Mark."* Thus it is possible that Mark himself is responsible for the passion as we know it and that there is no need to posit an earlier version of the passion story.

Kelber has developed this hypothesis further in *The Oral and the Written Gospel*.[27] His investigations of oral tradition and written Gospel (textuality) lead him to conclude that the movement from the oral to the written stage in the formation of the Gospel was not as smooth and linear as the form critics supposed. To the contrary, the written Gospel was the evangelist's way of putting an end to the creative development which characterized the oral tradition. In the case of Mark's Gospel, the evangelist was opposing many of the Christological ideas present in the oral tradition and substituting his own.

> While it is widely conceded that the written gospel may be the early Christian movement's most significant contribution to literature, we have tended to operate on the assumption that the written gospel was but a surrogate for oral proclamation. But we cannot flatter ourselves with the path-breaking significance of the written gospel and simultaneously insist on its unbroken connectedness with tradition.[28]

Thus Kelber contends that Mark's Gospel signals a creative stage which involves a distancing and alienation from the tradition which preceded it.

While most authors are convinced that the passion narrative developed at an early stage in the oral tradition and was soon put to writing, Kelber contends that the oral tradition had little interest in the sufferings and death of Jesus because it was primarily concerned with Jesus' active life as teacher and healer. The literary nature of Mark's passion narrative argues for a later period, a stage which reflects Mark's preoccupation with Jesus' death, the failure of the disciples, and the fall of the temple. In a word, the passion narrative does not derive from the earlier oral tradition; it is primarily Mark's own achievement, written in part to combat the Christological portrait of Jesus found in the oral tradition.

Like Fowler and Dewey, Kelber views Mark as a skilled literary figure. However, he goes further inasmuch as he understands the evangelist as a creative theologian opposing and correcting the traditions and sources he received. Mark does not merely inherit and arrange sources; his written Gospel puts an end to the oral tradition and creates a new universe, the Gospel of Mark. "With Mark a world was written into being by distanciation from oral dialogue and remembering."[29]

Mark as a Conservative Redactor

Not all authors agree that Mark was such a creative theologian. In Europe and Great Britain, several exegetes view the evangelist as a conservative redactor who respected the traditions passed on to him. Ernest Best espouses this position in an important article.[30] He argues that when faced with a piece of tradition, Mark did little to alter it internally. For example, although Mark's preferred titles for Jesus are Son of God, Son of Man, and Teacher, he does not alter titles such as the Holy One of God (1:24) or the Son of David (10:47,48) which he received from the tradition.

Mark's creativity consisted in placing "the tradition in his total context supplying audience, place, time and sequence and in the summaries he has written he has been quite obviously creative."[31] Thus it is better to think of him as an artist creating a collage rather than as an author. In a later work, Best modifies this position.

> A better illustration may be that of a composer who brings together folk songs or sea shanties to make a new unity. Just as each of the original tunes is clearly recognizable but each has also been subtly changed to accommodate to it what precedes and follows, so Mark created a new and exciting whole out of the material available to him in the tradition.[32]

Best can even say that Mark used the tradition creatively,[33] but he would not agree with Kelber that the evangelist rewrote the tradition in order to oppose or alter its original meaning. There is continuity between the oral tradition and Mark's written Gospel.[34]

Rudolf Pesch defends a more conservative position. He is convinced that in the past twenty years Mark's literary achievement has been overemphasized and his commitment to the Jesus tradition underrated.[35] Mark was the master of the tradition he received, but he was also a conservative redactor. His achievement was to order the material in the form of an historical presentation (*Geschichtsdarstellung*).[36] Mark is not an innovator but a compiler, arranger and adapter of tradition.[37] The speech and style of his work is almost identical to the style and speech of the tradition.[38] In effect, Mark's literary achievement is to be found in his conservative procedure which joins traditions into a narrative form. Through simple juxtaposition of traditions, intercalation of material, and the utilization of time and place, the evangelist has created a work which strikes the reader as an historical presentation.[39]

Conclusion

Despite the many investigations into Mark's Gospel, there is still no consensus regarding how it was composed. In fact, there is a fundamental disagreement between those who view the evangelist as a creative redactor who thoroughly rewrote the traditions he received and those who see him as a conservative redactor who arranged the traditions but respected their internal integrity. The impasse issues from the difficulty in determining with assurance Mark's sources and traditions. If this question could be answered satisfactorily, it would be possible to settle the dispute regarding the evangelist's use of his sources. Unfortunately, it seems less and less likely that the question of sources will be settled soon, if at all.

In face of this deadlock, many exegetes have turned to new methodologies such as rhetorical criticism and literary criticism, which go beyond a discussion of sources. However, here another danger arises: when the Gospel is studied on a purely literary level it may be set loose from its moorings in history. In itself, there is nothing wrong with a literary study of the Gospel, but if this is the *only* study of the Gospel, it will inevitably impoverish Gospel research.

For the moment there does not seem to be a clear direction in Markan studies. The newer, literary approaches have only begun and will continue to be pursued. But the more traditional questions of source criticism and the Gospel's formation have not been settled and must not be neglected.

5
The Narrative of Mark's Gospel

How can a Gospel as brief as Mark's produce such a flood of studies? How can a scholar read the secondary literature on the Gospel of Mark and still hope to say something original? In part the answer is found in new methodological approaches. Let me explain. In the nineteenth century NT critics were primarily interested in Mark's Gospel as an historical source for the life of Jesus. Consequently, they employed the methodology of source criticism in order to determine the historical reliability of the Gospel. At the beginning of this century, scholars were more interested in the life of the early Church. Therefore they applied the methodology of form criticism to the Gospel to discover what it reveals about the period between Jesus' death and the first written Gospel (30–70 A.D.). Then, in the middle of this century a new generation turned its attention to the evangelist and his theology. As a result, it applied the methodology of redaction criticism to Mark's Gospel. In a word, different methodologies have enabled scholars to read an old text anew.

Today Markan students continue to apply different methodologies to the Gospel in order to hear the text afresh. Thus some are applying the tools of social analysis to the text to obtain a clearer picture of the social structure and values behind the Gospel. Others are reading the text with the assistance of categories learned from anthropology, and still others work with the highly abstract categories provided by structural analysis. Most of these ventures have only begun.

In my opinion, however, the most fruitful direction in Markan studies so far has been opened by those scholars who are reading the Gospel in terms of literary and rhetorical criticism. Although the redaction critics of the 50s, 60s and 70s viewed Mark as an author and theologian, they often read the Gospel in a piecemeal fashion by concentrating primarily on the evangelist's supposed additions and alterations to the traditions he received. Thus there was a hidden bias that Markan theology was to be found *only* in those portions of the Gospel that the evangelist edited. Furthermore, redaction critics used the text as a *window* through which they could view the historical situation in which the Gospel was written.

The approach of literary and rhetorical critics is different. Such scholars do not focus on sources which lie behind the text. For them the text is a unity, no part being of more value than another merely because the evangelist may have edited it. Nor do such critics treat the text as a window through which they can view the world of the first century. The world with which they are concerned is the world presented by the story in the Gospel text. Thus their attention is upon the rhetorical techniques employed by the author to narrate the story.

In recent years there have been two approaches to the study of Mark as narrative. First, some scholars have tried to identify the rhetorical genre of the Gospel by comparing it with similar literature found in the Greco-Roman world of the first century. They argue that the Gospel should be read in the light of Greek tragedy or according to the model of Greek biography in which a philosopher gathers disciples and transmits his system of thought to them. A second approach employs the tools of contemporary literary criticism. Its proponents argue that since Mark is a narrative, it is capable of being analyzed like any other story in terms of plot, character development, narrative techniques, etc.

Although these approaches are different, they share a common assumption: the Gospel of Mark is a narrative which relates an intriguing story. Because of this, it should be read as a unified piece of literature, a story in which a narrator communicates to a reader. In this chapter we will examine both approaches.

The Gospel Narrative and Ancient Literature

Gilbert G. Bilezikian in *The Liberated Gospel*[1] has made the strongest argument that there are important similarities between the Gospel of Mark and Greek tragedy. From the beginning of his work, however, Bilezikian notes that Mark did not consciously undertake to write a Greek tragedy. Thus the Gospel remains a narrative and not a play composed for theatrical performance.[2] Nevertheless, Bilezikian contends that to give the Gospel shape, Mark imitated the model of Greek tragedy with which he and his contemporaries were familiar.

> His secret may well reside in the blending of variegated elements of episodic narrative into a harmoniously connected whole by means of the judicious incorporation of the most effective dramatic device ever discovered by man to penetrate the mysteries of the gods.[3]

Bilezikian's work presupposes that Mark is a Roman Gospel. On the basis of this assumption, he shows that although Greek tragedy first flourished in Athens, it rapidly spread throughout the Hellenized world. Most importantly, it came to Rome where it gave birth to Latin drama. Furthermore, there also developed a kind of tragedy long before and during Mark's time "written not for stage presentation, but simply for reading—as the Gospel was."[4] Among the authors of such tragedies was Mark's contemporary, Seneca. So Bilezikian contends that tragedies were being written and performed at Rome, and ordinary citizens such as Mark would have had access to their performance. Given this atmosphere, the influence of tragedy upon the composition of Mark's Gospel becomes a real possibility.

According to Bilezikian, the plot of Mark's Gospel contains the essential elements for tragedy as outlined by Aristotle in the *Poetics:* a complication, a crisis or a recognition scene, a denouement. Thus the Gospel may be outlined in the following manner:

1:1—8:26	The Complication
8:27—30	The Recognition Scene
8:31—16:8	The Denouement

In the first part of the Gospel (1:1–8:26), the complication arises when the human characters of the narrative cannot grasp Jesus' transcendent identity despite his mighty words and deeds. This complication, however, does not simply result from the inability of the human characters to understand Jesus. It derives from the very nature of his messiahship which *cannot* be understood until after his death and resurrection. Thus Jesus is the tragic victim of his own destiny to be the crucified Messiah.[5]

According to Aristotle, the transition from complication to denouement is the crisis. Here a climactic event takes place so that the action of the play can shift. This event often takes the form of a recognition scene in which the protagonist is recognized for who he truly is. In Mark's Gospel, according to Bilezikian, Peter's confession at Caesarea Philippi (8:27–30) is this crisis or recognition scene. Peter and the disciples finally recognize that Jesus is the Messiah. As a result, the action within the Gospel can take a new turn; the denouement begins.

In the complication phase the action of the plot focuses upon the identity of Jesus. Who is he? In the denouement (8:31–16:8) the action concentrates upon the accomplishment of Jesus' messianic task. Thus Mark rivets his attention upon three main lines of development in this phase: (1) the training of the disciples and their subsequent failure; (2) the success of Jesus' opponents in obtaining his death; (3) the final success of Jesus' messianic program.[6] In this last phase, therefore, Jesus teaches his disciples the doctrine of the crucified and risen Messiah as well as its implications for their own lives. He exposes the murderous designs of the religious leaders who eventually put him to death. Finally, despite this opposition he accomplishes his goal, and through the resurrection his messianic program comes to fruition.

For Bilezikian the complication-crisis-denouement pattern is clearly represented in Mark's Gospel. In itself this does not mean that the Gospel is a tragedy or that Mark intended to write a tragedy.[7] But according to Bilezikian, when composing the Gospel, Mark was influenced by one of the most popular and powerful modes of expression of his day, Greek tragedy.

The work of Benoit Standaert, *L'Évangile selon Marc*[8] is similar to Bilezikian's inasmuch as it looks to Greco-Roman rhetoric in order to understand Mark's narrative. Standaert also notices many aspects of Greek drama in Mark's Gospel, but his own work focuses more upon the compositional techniques of the evangelist, techniques drawn from ancient rhetoric. Among the most important is Mark's fondness for concentric or chiastic patterns whereby a central point is highlighted by being enclosed within outer, parallel members.

A   B   "C"   B   A

According to this pattern, the central point "C" is surrounded by parallel members, A–A and B–B. Through the use of such compositional techniques, Mark composed a highly structured narrative. Furthermore, employing conventional rhetorical forms, his

Gospel introduces the reader to a well defined problem and then leads the reader to the appointed goal. Following the rhetorical forms of the day, the Gospel manifests the following structure.

1:1–13	The *Prologue* in which the author introduces John and Jesus.
1:14–6:13	The *Narrative* in which the author presents the facts, the words and deeds of Jesus, which prepare for the *Argument*.
6:14–10:52	The *Argument* in which the author addresses the question of Jesus' identity and the conditions necessary for discipleship.
11:1–15:47	The *Denouement* in which the final tragic week of Jesus' life is recorded.
16:1–8	The *Epilogue* in which a messenger reveals to the women that Jesus is alive.

In the *Prologue,* Mark presents both John and Jesus to the reader. John is described in terms reminiscent of Elijah, while Jesus is depicted as a new Moses and a new Isaac. By the conclusion of the *Prologue,* therefore, the reader knows who Jesus is, what his relationship is to God, to history, and to the Scriptures. By contrast, the characters within the story which follows are not privy to this inside information. Thus the *Prologue* establishes a dramatic tension. Armed with the knowledge that the *Prologue* provides, the reader watches from a superior position as the characters within the story's first eight chapters struggle to discover what the reader already knows.[9]

The *Narration* (1:14–6:13) simply presents Jesus. Thus the narrator (the evangelist) describes and reports Jesus' words and activity so that the reader can form a more complete idea of who Jesus is. The facts presented in the *Narration* prepare for the next major part of the story, the *Argument,* when the narrator will make the case for Jesus' identity as the Messiah who must suffer and die.

According to Standaert, the *Narration* manifests a highly developed structure which can be outlined as follows:

(a)	1:14–15	The beginning of Jesus' preaching
	1:16–20	Call of the first disciples
	1:21–3:6	*First Section* (Day at Capernaum and five controversies)
(b)	3:7–12	Summary of Jesus' mission
	3:13–19	Call of the twelve disciples
	3:20–5:43	*Second Section* (conflict with family and scribes, parable discourse, miracles)
(c)	6:1–6a	Preaching of Jesus in his hometown
	6:6b–13	Mission of the twelve disciples

According to the outline, the two main sections are bracketed by three smaller units (a,b,c). Each of these smaller units is related to the other by the common themes of Jesus' preaching/mission and discipleship.

In the *Argument* (6:14–10:52) questions, discussions, persuasion, and practical exhortation abound. The opening verses (6:14–16) serve as the leitmotif of the *Argument* by raising the question, ''Who is Jesus?'' It provides three erroneous opinions (a prophet, Elijah, John the Baptist) which will be corrected by Peter's confession.

The *Argument* proceeds in three steps. In a first (6:30–8:21), dominated by the two accounts of the multiplication of the loaves, the disciples manifest their hardness of heart and inability to understand Jesus. The entire section is bracketed by false opinions regarding who Jesus is (6:14–16 and 8:27–28).

At the center of the *Argument* is a second step of twenty-five verses (8:27–9:13) which takes up and articulates the major themes of the *Argument:* Jesus' identity and the conditions necessary for discipleship. Finally, after a transition story (9:14–29), the third step in the *Argument* (9:30–10:45) presents a series of instructions on various aspects of community life: the question of precedence, the strong and the weak, family questions, riches, desires for promotion. Like the *Narration,* the *Argument* manifests a complex structure.

6:14–16	Introduction (Who is Jesus?)
6:17–29	Transition story (death of John)
6:30–8:21	*First Step* (multiplication of loaves and misunderstanding of disciples)
8:22–26	Transition story (Who is Jesus?)
8:27–9:13	*Second Step* (recognition scene)
9:14–29	Transition story (expulsion of a demon)
9:30–10:45	*Third Step* (following the Son of Man)
10:46–52	Transition story (blind Bartimaeus)

The *Denouement* (11:1–15:47) takes place in and around Jerusalem, and the events occur during the course of a week. Like the *Argument,* the *Denouement* has three major steps. In the first (11:1–12:44), Jesus comes to the city of Jerusalem and its temple where he confronts the religious authorities. In the second (13:1–37), he delivers a long discourse. This discourse mirrors a technique known from ancient drama whereby the protagonist pronounces a last speech before dying or leaving the scene. Finally the passion (14:1–15:47) is the third step. By it the protagonist carries out his appointed destiny. The denouement can be outlined as follows:

11:1–12:40	*First Step* (Jesus in Jerusalem and the temple to confront religious leaders)
12:41–44	Transition story (the widow's mite)

13:1–37   *Second Step* (farewell discourse)
14:1–15:41   *Third Step* (passion)
15:42–47   Transition (burial of Jesus)

The *Epilogue* (16:1–8) consists of the story of the empty tomb. A young man (the messenger in Greek drama) announces the resurrection to the women and thereby calls the reader to follow Jesus to Galilee—that is, on the way of discipleship.

Like Bilezikian, Standaert sees Mark's Gospel as a drama written according to the rules of classical rhetoric. The original setting for the Gospel, according to Standaert, was the Easter vigil of the Roman Church in which the Gospel narrative served as a summons to those about to be baptized to follow the risen Lord. While many would not agree with Standaert on this last point, most would concur with his judgment that the Gospel was intended to be *heard* as a unified narrative.

The work of Vernon Robbins, *Jesus the Teacher,*[10] is unlike those studied above inasmuch as it proposes a different genre for understanding Mark's Gospel. According to Robbins, ''the Gospel of Mark partakes of the form of a biography that depicts a disciple-gathering teacher—from the high point of his career to his death.''[11] Robbins argues that Mark's Gospel played a significant role in early Christianity because it was able to integrate Jewish messianic expectations with a concept known and esteemed in Greco-Roman culture: the disciple-gathering teacher who transmits his system of thought to his disciples and demonstrates its worth by dying for it. Robbins writes: ''The Gospel of Mark was preserved because it perpetuated an image of Jesus, an understanding of discipleship, and a teaching/learning cycle compatible with ideology in Mediterranean society.''[12]

To substantiate his case, he points to Xenophon's *Memorabilia,* a loosely connected account of Socrates' actions and conversations. It describes the ''role of the religio-ethical teacher who gathers disciple-companions in order to transmit to them the system of thought and action that he himself embodies.''[13] According to Robbins, Mark drew from both the Israelite prophetic tradition and the Greco-Roman tradition of the disciple-gathering teacher in order to present Jesus, the Jewish Messiah, in a fashion that would be understandable to the Mediterranean world.

With the genre of the disciple-gathering teacher in mind, Robbins presents Mark's narrative of Jesus in three phases: a phase which initiates discipleship (1:14–3:6), a teaching and learning phase (3:7–12:44), and a phase of farewell and separation from the teacher (13:1–15:47).[14]

The initial phase (1:14–3:6) establishes Jesus' identity as a teacher who gathers disciples. Jesus calls his first disciples and they follow him, but he does not yet explain his system of thought to them.

The middle phase (3:7–12:44) is the most detailed and consists of four stages. In the first (3:7–5:43) Jesus begins to introduce the basic details of his system of thought to his disciples. In the second (6:1–8:26) his disciples are able to perform most of the activities characteristic of his ministry, yet they do not fully comprehend his system of thought. In the third stage (8:27–10:45) there are a series of conflicts between Jesus and his disciples over the central dimensions of his system of thought. Finally in the fourth (10:46–12:44) the disciples respectfully accompany Jesus to Jerusalem. The tension manifested in the third stage disappears, and Jesus publicly discusses issues of general concern while the disciples observe.

The final phase of the teacher-disciple relationship is one of farewell and death (13:1–15:47). It unfolds in two stages. In the first (13:1–37) Jesus delivers a lengthy discourse to four of his disciples to prepare them for his departure. And in the second (14:1–15:47) he accepts arrest, trial, and death, thereby proving the worth of his system of thought.

Robbins' hypothesis about the genre which influenced Mark leads him to interpret the Gospel narrative differently from Bilezikian and Standaert. Nonetheless, he would agree with them that the Gospel needs to be read as a unified narrative constructed according to the principles of ancient rhetoric. Though these authors do not concur about the exact genre which influenced the evangelist most strongly, they have demonstrated that Mark can be read as a story and that his story has been constructed by an author aware of rhetorical techniques.

The Gospel Narrative and Contemporary Literary Criticism

A second approach to Mark as narrative has been undertaken by those scholars who apply the tools of contemporary literary criticism to the Gospel. We have already mentioned some of them (Dewey, Fowler, Kingsbury, Tannehill, Juel). All of them share a common conviction that since the Gospel is a unified narrative, it can be analyzed in terms of its plot, characterization, and discourse in the same manner that literary critics study novels and short stories. Since literary critics have already shaped the tools for such analysis, New Testament scholars borrow from their methodology.

One of the first efforts to apply literary criticism to Mark's Gospel was undertaken by Norman R. Petersen in a small volume entitled *Literary Criticism for New Testament Critics.*[15] In that work Petersen explains the differences between redaction criticism and literary criticism. He observes that while redaction critics made important gains over the form critics by correctly recognizing Mark as an author and theologian, they were victims of their own designs inasmuch as they sought ''to find the integrity of a text in the theological motivation for its redaction.''[16] That is, redaction critics were primarily interested in the changes and alterations that the evangelist made to the tradition he received but did not fully appreciate the text as a literary work. Thus it was not unusual for redaction critics to emphasize certain verses as more important than others because they were thought to be added or edited by the evangelist.

By contrast, literary criticism does not concern itself with the question of sources or redaction. For the literary critic the text is a whole, a world which once created by the author takes on an existence of its own. "The total meaning of a work of art can not be defined merely in terms of its meaning for the author and his contemporaries."[17] So Petersen and other literary critics argue that the text should not simply be understood as a window through which the reader views the historical author and his or her contemporaries. The text is a world in itself apart from the author and the original audience for whom the author wrote. It is a kind of mirror in which the reader sees himself or herself reflected in the world of the story.

To clarify this, Petersen speaks of the referential fallacy which consists of thinking of the text as if it were a direct representation of the real world.[18] Applied to Mark's Gospel, the referential fallacy means treating the Gospel text as if it were merely a reflection of historical reality so that the characters of the text are direct representations of their historical counterparts.

To be sure one can read the Gospel in order to discover something about the historical Jesus and the early Church, *but literary critics do not.* When reading a text, they place the question of history in abeyance. The characters within the text are not studied in terms of their historical referents, e.g., Jesus, the disciples. Instead they are examined as characters who live and exist in the world which the narrator has created. Understood in this way, the text is viewed as a self-contained universe in much the same way that a portrait by an artist is a self-contained universe. To be sure the characters which people one of Brugel's paintings, for example, represent real people who lived in Brugel's time. But now, within the painting, these characters exist in an autonomous universe which the artist has created. It is this universe and these characters with which the literary critic is concerned, not their historical counterparts.

While this procedure may seem strange, it is something we do when we turn on a television drama. For example, the characters of a television program such as "Dallas" live in a self-contained universe created by the scriptwriter, and yet to most of us these characters are as real as the people in our neighborhood. We discuss their problems and offer them advice. We rarely think of them as fictional; they are real to us because we allow ourselves to enter their universe each time we tune in to a new episode. For sixty minutes we suspend our knowledge that JR is Larry Hagman and accept him for the person he is in the world of "Dallas."

The attempt to read Mark as a story is something similar. Literary critics do not deny the historical value of the Gospel; they are simply not concerned with it when they read the text (redaction critics are). Instead they are interested in the literary world which the text of Mark creates. Who are the characters within this world? How do they interact with each other? What are the conflicts which allow the plot to develop, and how are these conflicts resolved? Inasmuch as Mark is a story, it deserves a careful reading as a story. After such a literary investigation the exegete is in a stronger position to discover what the text has to say about the historical Jesus and the early Church since he or she will be able to distinguish between the evangelist's literary and historical intentions. Petersen writes,

> the literary character of Mark's narrative must be understood before its evidential value can be assessed. Literary criticism would thus be either a fundamental stage of historical criticism or a stage which in this respect must precede historical criticism.[19]

In a sense the nineteenth century search for the historical Jesus was misguided not because the project was wrong but because its proponents had not yet understood the literary characteristics of the text with which they were dealing.

A more recent literary critical analysis, *Mark as Story,*[20] has been produced by a New Testament scholar, David Rhoads, in collaboration with an English scholar, Donald Michie. They note that every narrative can be viewed from two vantage points.[21] First, there is the story, *what* the narrative is about. Here the basic elements are events, characters, and setting. Second, there is the rhetoric of discourse, that is, *how* the story is told. Employing this distinction, they analyze Mark's narrative in terms of rhetoric (how), setting, plot, and characters (what).

Perhaps the single most important rhetorical device of the narrative is the employment of an omniscient narrator, a narrator who knows the thoughts and feelings of all the characters within the story and is not bound by time and space. Although the reader does not always advert to the narrator's presence, it is the narrator who leads the reader through the story, showing what he wills. Thus the reader ''comes to trust the narrator as a reliable guide in the world of the story.''[22] and ''to rely on the narrator to provide reliable commentary on the story.''[23]

Although the narrator often seems withdrawn and neutral, literary critics stress that every narrator represents an ideological point of view, i.e., a system of values. In certain sophisticated narratives, the author may employ a narrator whose ideological point of view is erroneous and unreliable, but in Mark's Gospel the narrator is a reliable guide inasmuch as the narrator's ideological point of view or system of values is aligned with that of Jesus, i.e., ''thinking the things of God'' (8:33, my translation). So when the narrator informs the reader who Jesus is (the Son of God) and what his destiny is (suffering and death), the reader can trust what is said. In other words, careful attention to what the narrator of the story says will instruct the reader how to understand the story properly.

While the primary rhetorical device of Mark's Gospel is the

employment of the reliable, omniscient narrator, the evangelist uses many other devices to lead the reader through the story world, e.g., repetition, questions, placing episodes in concentric patterns, riddles, quotations from Scripture. But among the most important is Mark's use of irony, especially verbal irony, ''when a speaker self-consciously says one thing but means the opposite.''[24] Thus in the passion the soldiers mock Jesus as a messianic fraud by reviling him as the King of the Jews. However, thanks to the reliable commentary of the narrator the reader knows that what the soldiers say in derision is true; Jesus is the messianic King. Through the analysis of the use of these and other rhetorical devices, Rhoads and Michie demonstrate that although the Gospel is a simple story it is told with artistic grace.

When Rhoads and Michie turn to *what* the story of Mark's Gospel is about, they deal with setting, plot, and characters. In the Gospel there are several settings against which the overall movement of the Gospel and the plot develop, e.g., the Jordan River, the desert, the sea, the mountains. However, the basic setting is provided by Jesus' movements through Galilee and his great journey to Jerusalem. This journey ''creates a funneling effect for the whole story. In the first half of the story the movement ranges widely throughout all Galilee and beyond. Then the direction narrows in toward Jerusalem, finally ending there.''[25]

The various settings of the Gospel are the background for the plot which is worked out through a series of conflicts with demonic forces, nature, the religious authorities, and the disciples. While Jesus overcomes the demonic forces and even nature (stilling the storm), his most difficult conflicts are with the human characters in the narrative, especially the religious leaders and disciples, since they can choose for themselves. It is through these conflicts that the plot unfolds.

The conflict with the religious leaders, as the parable of the vineyard shows, arises because they have ruled for themselves rather than for God. Jesus comes as God's beloved Son to reestablish God's rule. This conflict between Jesus and the leaders is finally resolved when the religious authorities obtain their wish to put Jesus to death. Ironically, however, their wish coincides with God's will for Jesus. By delivering Jesus to Pilate the authorities unwittingly help bring about God's destiny for his Messiah.

The conflict with the disciples is different, and according to Rhoads and Michie it never comes to a successful resolution within the plotted time of the story. The disciples want and try to be generous followers of Jesus, but they resist his journey to Jerusalem where he must suffer and die. Thus the conflict experienced by the disciples is between loyalty to Jesus and their own desire for personal survival. Whether the disciples ever resolve this conflict remains an open question since the Gospel concludes with the women leaving the tomb without telling the disciples the message of Jesus' resurrection.[26] Nonetheless the reader is assured that when God's rule is finally established all conflicts will ultimately be resolved by the Son of Man.

In addition to setting and plot, Rhoads and Michie study characterization (the manner in which the narrator brings the characters to life) as a constituent element of story. They note that Jesus and the disciples are portrayed as *round* characters (characters with changing and predictable traits who are complex and unpredictable), whereas the religious authorities are *flat* characters (characters with fewer, usually consistent, traits who are predictable). Thus Jesus is a round character because he has many and varied traits (authority, integrity, faith, selflessness), whereas his opponents have a few consistent traits which stand in opposition to God's rule. ''They are self-serving, preoccupied with their own importance, afraid to lose their status and power, and willing to destroy to keep them.''[27] The disciples are round characters because of their conflicting traits. ''On the one hand, they are loyal and courageous, with a capacity for sacrifice and enough fascination with Jesus to follow him. On the other hand, they are afraid, self-centered and dense, preoccupied with their own status and power.''[28]

At this juncture it is important not to commit the referential fallacy. Literary critics do not equate these characters (Jesus, his opponents, the disciples) to their historical counterparts. These character descriptions, therefore, should not be understood as descriptions of the historical Jesus, his opponents, and the disciples. Rather the literary critic is concerned with Jesus, the opponents, and the disciples as characters within Mark's narrative world.

Summary

The literary-critical study of Mark's Gospel has made two important contributions. First, it has aided NT scholars to view the Gospel as a unified story, a literary work rather than as a collection of disparate traditions. The Gospel of Mark is an excellent story, replete with drama and irony. No matter how the Gospel was originally composed, it now functions as a unified narrative. Perhaps the best evidence for this is the consistent manner in which the author employs an omniscient, reliable narrator to lead the reader through the story world.

Second, literary criticism has made NT students more aware of the rhetorical devices present in Mark's narrative. On first reading, the Gospel appears to be a simple, even clumsy story. But on closer examination it reveals a series of sophisticated rhetorical devices ranging from concentric patterns to a masterful use of irony.

It may well be that the most profitable agenda for Markan studies lies in the direction set by literary criticism. J. D. Kingsbury has already made a significant study of Mark's Christology by employing this method. Surely many other questions need to be reexamined in light of this newest methodology. However, as I cautioned in the last chapter, an exclusively literary-critical approach to the Gospel presents the danger of dislodging the Gospel from its historical moorings. Sooner or later NT scholars must address the historical questions surrounding the Gospel.

In the nineteenth century these questions were studied under the rubric of the search for the historical Jesus. But as I mentioned earlier, scholars of that era did not fully appreciate the literary nature of the work they investigated. They were primarily interested in Mark as a window onto the first century. I submit that their investigations would have been more profitable had they begun with a literary-critical study and then moved to the historical questions for which they sought answers. In our own age, once the text has been understood on literary-critical grounds, it will be our responsibility to return to such historical questions.

Conclusion

So what are they saying about the Gospel according to Mark? At the end of this survey I suspect that not a few readers are puzzled and even frustrated. Markan scholars seem to be divided over the central issues of this brief document: its setting, its Christology, its view of the disciples, the nature of its composition. Was Mark written at Rome or in Palestine? Is the evangelist attacking a false Christology within his community, or is he simply concerned to present Jesus as the Son of God? Did Mark view the disciples as adversaries, or was he using the example of their failure to instruct his readers about the true nature of discipleship? What are the sources employed by the evangelist in composing the Gospel? Can they be delimited with any certainty, or must we always remain in the realm of hypothesis?

The reader seeking definitive answers will be disappointed. There simply is no consensus among Markan scholars about these and other important issues. Nor is there likely to be in the immediate future. In part, the document with which we are dealing does not provide us with the information we need.

By far the most elusive questions concern the composition of Mark's Gospel and its historical setting. All speculation regarding the sources for the Gospel seems destined to remain on the level of hypotheses. It is impossible to separate tradition from redaction with absolute certainty. It is not surprising, therefore, that the pursuit of sources is on the wane, and more and more scholars are employing a literary-critical approach which deals with the Gospel as a unified narrative.

While there is a strong tradition that Mark's Gospel was written at Rome, and while there are many indications within the Gospel that this is the case, it remains possible that the Gospel was composed elsewhere. It does not appear, however, that any of these new theories (Galilee, Syria) has brought forth decisive evidence which has yet won a consensus in the scholarly world. Thus, although I continue to favor the traditional Roman hypothesis, I admit the need to be genuinely open to other possibilities.

The questions of discipleship and Christology remain disputed, and it is still too early to speak of a consensus. Nonetheless I have a certain sense that those hypotheses founded upon the assumption of a theological crisis within the Markan community are on the wane. I am less and less convinced by theories which view the disciples as representatives of a false theological position or by hypotheses which see Mark as combating a false Christology.

Perhaps the basic difficulty in Markan studies can be traced back to the nature of the evangelist's redactional activity. Was Mark a creative writer and theologian who altered and even challenged the traditions he received? Or was Mark a conservative redactor and theologian who basically reverenced and cherished the traditions he inherited? Those who espouse the first position tend to interpret the evangelist's view of Christology and discipleship in a more radical fashion. They are inclined to posit heresies and difficulties within the community against which the evangelist reacted. On the other hand, those who view Mark as a conservative redactor see a greater continuity between the evangelist and his tradition and less need to posit such theories.

By now my own prejudices are apparent. I view Mark as a Roman Gospel written to present Jesus as the messianic Son of God. I do not think that Mark was combating a false Christology, nor am I convinced that he polemicized against the disciples. The failure of the disciples serves as a pastoral example. In brief I understand Mark as a conservative redactor and theologian who preserved the traditions he received.

Despite the lack of consensus in Markan scholarship, there have been some genuine advances. Anyone who has read through this book has become aware that the cross and death of Jesus play the central role in Mark's theology. It is to the credit of Markan scholarship that it has resolutely struggled with Wrede's messianic secret, a theological problem which has shown them that the cross stands at the center of Mark's theology. It is to the credit of Markan scholarship that it has struggled with the titles Son of God and Son of Man and discovered that neither can be understood apart from the cross. It is to the credit of Markan scholarship that it has doggedly pursued Mark's view of the disciples and discovered that in this Gospel discipleship cannot be grasped apart from the cross.

Where is Markan scholarship going? Is there a clear direction for the future? From one point of view the answer is ''no.'' Markan scholars have followed and continue to pursue diverse paths. There are too many opposing views within the community of Markan scholarship to speak of a clear or unified direction for the future. Nonetheless, one path that needs to be pursued is the continued study of Mark as narrative. Like any story, Mark's narrative can be read and reread from different angles. A deeper appreciation of Mark's Gospel as story, therefore, should be part of the immediate agenda. When that agenda has been fulfilled, perhaps we can return to the question raised by the nineteenth century: Who is Jesus of Nazareth?

Notes

1. The Setting for Mark's Gospel

1. For a discussion of the three stages in the Gospel tradition see the Biblical Commission's Instruction on the Historical Truth of the Gospels. The text, and a commentary on it, can be found in Joseph A. Fitzmyer, *A Christological Catechism: New Testament Answers* (New York: Paulist, 1982).

2. Willi Marxsen (*Mark the Evangelist: Studies on the Redaction History of the Gospel* [Nashville: Abingdon, 1969]) was among the first to investigate Mark's redactional activity and to formulate an hypothesis about the community for which the evangelist wrote.

3. For a clear exposition of the different "churches" represented in the NT, see Raymond E. Brown, *The Churches the Apostles Left Behind* (New York: Paulist, 1984).

4. Vincent Taylor (*The Gospel According to Mark: The Greek Text with Introduction, Notes, and Indexes*, 2nd ed. [New York: St. Martin's Press, 1966] pp. 1–8) provides a convenient collection of the most important patristic texts.

5. The translation is taken from Eusebius, *The History of the Church from Christ to Constantine*, trans. with an intro. by G. A. Williamson (Penguin Classics, 1965, p. 152) Book 3, par 39.

6. Kurt Niederwimmer, "Johannes Markus und die Frage

nach dem Verfasser des zweiten Evangeliums,'' *ZNW* 58 (1967) 172–88.

7. Martin Hengel, *Studies in the Gospel of Mark* (Philadelphia: Fortress, 1985).

8. *Ibid.*, p. 47.

9. *Ibid.*, p. 52.

10. *Ibid.*, p. 46.

11. Ernest Best, *Mark the Gospel as Story* (Studies of the New Testament and Its World; Edinburgh: T. & T. Clark, 1983).

12. *Ibid.*, p. 144.

13. S. G. F. Brandon, *Jesus and the Zealots: A Study of the Political Factor in Primitive Christianity* (Manchester University Press, 1967). Brandon has presented the same arguments in his article, "The Date of the Markan Gospel," *NTS* 7 (1961–62) 126–41.

14. *Ibid.*, p. 242.

15. *Ibid.*, p. 243.

16. *Ibid.*, p. 265.

17. Brandon's argument has been adapted by Charles Masson (*L'Évangile de Marc et l'Église de Rome* [Bibliotheque Théologique; Neuchâtel: Delachaux et Niestle, 1968]). Masson argues that the canonical Gospel of Mark is an abbreviated and greatly altered form of an earlier Markan Gospel used in Rome. The purpose of this abbreviated Gospel was to dissociate the Gospel of Jesus Christ from Judaism and Jerusalem, and to calm the apocalyptic expectations which troubled the Roman Church.

18. Benoit Standaert, *L'Évangile selon Marc: Composition et Genre Litteraire* (Nijmegen: Stichting Studentenpers, 1978). This work represents Standaert's doctoral dissertation. A more popular presentation of his ideas can be found in *L'Évangile selon Marc: Commentaire* (Lire la Bible; Paris: Les Editions du Cerf, 1983).

19. There are, of course, internal arguments that Mark composed his Gospel from Rome. Among the arguments usually cited

are his use of Latin loan words and his use of the Roman method of reckoning time. For a brief summary of these arguments see William L. Lane, *The Gospel According to Mark: The English Text with Introduction, Exposition and Notes* (The New International Commentary on the New Testament; Grand Rapids; Eerdmans, 1974) 24–25.

20. See note 2.

21. *Ibid.*, p. 67.

22. Pella is not in Galilee, but Marxsen argues that Mark does not define the land of Galilee narrowly. Therefore, Pella can be considered part of the land of Galilee.

23. Werner H. Kelber, *The Kingdom of Mark: A New Place and a New Time* (Philadelphia: Fortress, 1974).

24. *Ibid.*, p. 130.

25. Howard Clark Kee, *Community of the New Age: Studies in Mark's Gospel* (Philadelphia: Westminster, 1977).

26. *Ibid.*, p. 97.

27. *Ibid.*, p. 105.

28. For a thorough discussion of the internal evidence see Standaert, *L'Évangile selon Marc: Composition et Genre Litteraire*, pp. 465–95.

29. *Ibid.*, pp. 470–72.

2. The Christology of Mark's Gospel

1. Although most modern translations include the longer ending of Mark (16:9–20) in which the risen Lord appears to his disciples, the best manuscripts conclude the Gospel with the account of the empty tomb (16:1–8). Most scholars agree that this is how the evangelist ended his story. The attempts within the manuscript tradition to provide the Gospel with another, more satisfying ending indicate that the original conclusion was disturbing to many readers of the Gospel in the second and third centuries as it is to us today. They, like us, were accustomed to an ending of

Jesus' life which included a resurrection appearance. That Mark does not provide such an ending makes his Gospel unsettling.

2. For an interesting list of points of contact between Mark and some aspects of contemporary Christology, see M. Eugene Boring, "The Christology of Mark: Hermeneutical Issues for Systematic Theology," *Semeia* 30 (1984) 125–55, esp. pp. 150–53.

3. *Ibid.*, pp. 148–50.

4. David Rhoads and Donald Michie, *Mark as Story: An Introduction to the Narrative of a Gospel* (Philadelphia: Fortress, 1982); Norman Petersen, *Literary Criticism for New Testament Critics* (Philadelphia: Fortress, 1978), pp. 49–80; Robert C. Tannehill, "The Gospel of Mark as Narrative Christology," *Semeia* 16 (1979) 57–95.

5. Boring, "The Christology of Mark," p. 133.

6. *Ibid.*, p. 137.

7. Tannehill, "The Gospel of Mark," p. 57.

8. First published in 1901, the book has been translated into English, *The Messianic Secret* (London: James Clark, 1971).

9. For a brief presentation of Wrede's thesis and the discussion following it, see James L. Blevins, *The Messianic Secret in Markan Research 1901–1976* (Washington: University Press of America, 1981); Jack Dean Kingsbury, *The Christology of Mark's Gospel* (Philadelphia: Fortress, 1983), pp. 1–23; Christopher Tuckett, "Introduction: The Problem of the Messianic Secret," in *The Messianic Secret,* ed. Christopher Tuckett (Issues in Religion and Theology 1; Philadelphia: Fortress, 1983), pp. 1–28.

10. Blevins, *The Messianic Secret,* p. 10.

11. Ulrich Luz, "The Secrecy Motif and the Marcan Christology," *ZNW* 56 (1965) 9–30, reprinted in Tuckett, *The Messianic Secret,* pp. 75–96. My references are to the Tuckett volume.

12. *Ibid.*, p. 79.

13. *Ibid.*, p. 85.

14. A summary of Räisänen's conclusion from *Das "Mes-*

siasgeheimnis" im Markusevangelium (Schriften der Finnischen Exegetischen Gesellschaft 28; Helsinki: Länsi-Suomi, 1976) can be found in Tuckett, *The Messianic Secret,* pp. 132–40.

15. *Ibid.,* p. 132.

16. *Ibid.,* p. 135.

17. For an exposition and critique of this approach, see Kingsbury, *The Christology of Mark's Gospel,* pp. 25–45.

18. For a description of the Hellenistic divine man, see Paul J. Achtemeier, "Gospel Miracle Tradition and the Divine Man," *Int* 26 (1972) 174–97; Hans Dieter Betz, "Jesus as Divine Man," in *Jesus and the Historian: Written in Honor of Ernest Cadman Colwell,* ed. F. Thomas Trotter (Philadelphia: Westminster, 1968), pp. 114–33, esp. p. 116; Ludger Schenke, *Glory and the Way of the Cross: The Gospel of Mark* (Herald Biblical Booklets; Chicago: Franciscan Herald Press, 1972), pp.40–49; and Theodore Weeden, *Mark: Traditions in Conflict* (Philadelphia: Fortress, 1971), p. 55.

19. Thus H. D. Betz ("Jesus as Divine Man") writes, "Obviously, Mark radically criticizes and *corrects* the Christology of his sources . . . " (p. 124). Weeden (*Traditions in Conflict*) asserts, "The only points at which Mark will allow a *theios-aner* title to stand unsilenced is when the title has been properly *reinterpreted* in terms of Son-of-man christology" (p. 155). And Perrin ("The Christology of Mark: A Study in Methodology," *JR* 51 [1971] 173–87, reprinted in *The Interpretation of Mark,* ed. William Telford [Issues in Religion and Theology 7; Philadelphia: Fortress, 1985], pp. 95–108. My references are to this volume) notes, "He is concerned with *correcting* a false Christology prevalent in his church" (p. 99). [The emphasis in these quotations is mine.]

20. Weeden's thesis is summarized in an article, "The Heresy That Necessitated Mark's Gospel," *ZNW* 59 (1968) 145–58 which has been reprinted in the volume edited by Telford, *The*

Interpretation of Mark, pp 64–77. My references are to this volume.

21. Weeden, *Tradition in Conflict*, p. 55.

22. *Ibid.*, p. 52.

23. *Ibid.*, pp. 160–61 for a description of these opponents.

24. *Ibid.*, p. 165.

25. *Ibid.*, chapter 6.

26. "The Creative Use of the Son of Man Traditions by Mark," in *A Modern Pilgrimage in New Testament Christology* (Philadelphia: Fortress, 1974), pp. 84–93; "The Christology of Mark: A Study of Methodology," reprinted in Telford, *The Interpretation of Mark*, pp. 95–108; "The High Priest's Question and Jesus' Answer (Mark 14:61–62)," in *The Passion in Mark: Studies on Mark 14–16*, ed. Werner H. Kelber (Philadelphia: Fortress, 1976), pp. 80–95.

27. Perrin, "The Christology of Mark," p. 99.

28. *Ibid.*, p. 100.

29. The references can be found in Perrin, "The High Priest's Question," pp. 83–86.

30. Whether or not Son of Man should be called a title is disputed. See Kingsbury, *The Christology of Mark*, pp. 157–179. Perrin recognizes that properly speaking it is not a confessional title since only Jesus employs it. See "The Christology of Mark," p. 100.

31. Perrin, "The Christology of Mark," p. 100.

32. Perrin, "The High Priest's Question," p. 89.

33. For an important summary of this reaction see Jack Dean Kingsbury, "The 'Divine Man' as the Key to Mark's Christology—The End of an Era?" *Int* 35 (1981) 243–57.

34. Otto Betz, "The Concept of the So-Called 'Divine Man' in Mark's Christology," in *Studies in New Testament and Early Christian Literature: Essays in Honor of Allen Wikgren*, ed. by D. E. Aune (Leiden: Brill, 1972), pp. 229–40; and Carl H. Hol-

laday, *Theios Aner in Hellenistic–Judaism: A Critique of the Use of This Category in New Testament Christology* (SBLDS 40; Missoula, Montana: Scholars Press, 1977).

35. Carl R. Kazmierski, *Jesus, the Son of God: A Study of the Markan Tradition and Its Redaction by the Evangelist* (Forschung zur Bibel 33; Würzburg: Echter Verlag, 1979), p. 160.

36. Donald Juel, *Messiah and Temple: The Trial of Jesus in the Gospel of Mark* (SBLDS 31; Missoula, Montana: Scholars Press, 1977); Jack Dean Kingsbury, *The Christology of Mark's Gospel*; Frank J. Matera, *The Kingship of Jesus: Composition and Theology in Mark 15* (SBLDS 66; Chico, CA, 1982); and Hans-Jörg Steichele, *Der leidende Sohn Gottes: Eine Untersuchung einiger alttestamentlicher Motive in der Christologie des Markusevangeliums* (Biblische Untersuchungen 14; Regensburg: Friedrich Pustet, 1980).

37. Betz, "The Concept of the So-Called 'Divine Man,' " p. 232.

38. *Ibid.*, p. 240.

39. Holladay, *The Theios Aner*, p. 237.

40. *Ibid.*, p. 238.

41. *Ibid.*, p. 238.

42. Kazmierski, *Jesus, the Son of God*, p. 211.

43. *Ibid.*, pp. 67–68, 71.

44. My own work tries to show that Mark is primarily responsible for the composition of chapter 15 and that he composed this chapter in terms of the theme of Jesus' kingship. I argue that Son of God in 15:39 should be interpreted in terms of this royal messianism.

45. Juel, *Messiah and Temple*, pp. 77–125.

46. *Ibid.*, p. 92.

47. Kingsbury, *The Christology of Mark's Gospel*, p. 145.

48. *Ibid.*, p. 147.

49. *Ibid.*, p. 21.

3. The Disciples in Mark's Gospel

1. The relationship of the twelve to the disciples is one of the most difficult problems in Markan studies. It is discussed at the end of this chapter. I understand the twelve as a core group within the larger group of the disciples. While all that is said of the disciples can be applied to the twelve, not necessarily everything said of the twelve can be applied to the disciples. On the whole, however, Mark does not make a great distinction between the two groups.

2. These categories are found in the essay by William Telford, "Introduction: The Gospel of Mark," in *The Interpretation of Mark,* ed. William Telford (Issues in Religion and Theology 7; Philadelphia: Fortress, 1985), pp. 24–25.

3. Joseph B. Tyson, "The Blindness of the Disciples in Mark," *JBL* 80 (1961) 261–68, reprinted in *The Messianic Secret,* ed. Christopher Tuckett (Issues in Religion and Theology 1; Philadelphia: Fortress, 1983), pp. 35–43. My references are to this volume.

4. *Ibid.,* p. 37.

5. Etienne Trocmé, *The Formation of the Gospel according to Mark* (Philadelphia: Westminster, 1975). The book was originally published in 1963 in French, *La formation de l'Évangile selon Marc.*

6. *Ibid.,* p. 214.

7. *Ibid.,* p. 183.

8. Trocmé does not include chapters 14–16 in his outline since he believes that they were a later addition to the original Gospel of Mark.

9. Werner H. Kelber, *Mark's Story of Jesus* (Philadelphia: Fortress, 1979).

10. *Ibid.,* p. 88.

11. Kelber developed his thesis at greater length in *The*

Kingdom in Mark: A New Place and a New Time (Philadelphia: Fortress, 1974).

12. *Mark's Story of Jesus*, p. 52.

13. Ernest Best, *Following Jesus: Discipleship in the Gospel of Mark* (Journal for the Study of the New Testament Supplement Series 4; Sheffield: University of Sheffield, 1981), p. 12.

14. *Ibid.*

15. Karl-Georg Reploh, *Markus-Lehrer der Gemeinde: Eine redaktionsgeschichtliche Studie zu den Jungerperikopen des Markus-Evangeliums* (Stuttgarter Biblische Monographien 9; Stuttgart: Katholisches Bibelwerk, 1969).

16. Camille Focant, "L'Incompréhension des Disciples dans le deuxième Évangile," *RB* 82 (1985) 161–85. The texts studied are 4:13,40–41; 5:31; 6:37,51c–52; 7:18; 8:4,16–21,32–33; 9:5–6,19,32; 10:24,32; 14:37–41.

17. Robert C. Tannehill, "The Disciples in Mark: The Function of a Narrative Role," *JR* 57 (1977) 386–405, reprinted in *The Interpretation of Mark,* pp. 134–57. My citations are from *JR*.

18. *Ibid.,* p. 386.

19. *Ibid.,* p. 395.

20. R. P. Meye, *Jesus and the Twelve: Discipleship and Revelation in Mark's Gospel* (Grand Rapids: Eerdmans, 1968).

21. Klemens Stock, *Boten aus dem Mit-Ihm-Sein: Das Verhaltnis zwischen Jesus und den Zwolf nach Markus* (Analecta Biblica 70; Rome: Biblical Institute Press, 1975).

22. *Ibid.,* pp. 203–06.

23. Best, *Following Jesus,* pp. 208–45.

24. *Ibid.,* p. 219.

25. John R. Donahue, *The Theology and Setting of Discipleship in the Gospel of Mark* (1983 Pere Marquette Lecture; Milwaukee: Marquette University, 1983), especially pp. 31–56.

26. *Ibid.,* p. 53.

4. The Composition of Mark's Gospel

1. Part of the difficulty in establishing the exact meaning of the text from Papias is the Greek word *hermēneutēs* which can mean either "interpreter" or "translator." Thus the question arises: Did Mark merely translate what Peter said in Aramaic into Greek, or did he expand upon the apostle's words by interpreting them for the audience? The choice one makes here determines one's view of the evangelist as either merely a translator or as one who was on the way to becoming an author.

2. Not all scholars agree that Mark or the other evangelists initiated a new genre of literature. Some argue that the Gospels find their genre in Hellenistic romances or Greek biographies. At the present time the question of the Gospels' genre remains open.

3. Recently, Walter Schmithals (*Einleitung in die drei ersten Evangelien* [Berlin: de Gruyter, 1985], 410–31) has suggested that the canonical Gospel of Mark is based upon an earlier, artistic document which the author appears to have composed without a multiplicity of sources. Schmithals' theory runs counter to form critical analyses which posit several oral and written sources as the building material for each of the Gospels.

4. The work of Franz Neirynck (*Duality in Mark: Contributions to the Study of the Markan Reaction* [BETL 31; Louvain: Louvain University Press]) contends that a consistent literary style of duality pervades the whole of Mark's Gospel. If Neirynck is correct, then it is nearly impossible to determine Mark's sources with precision since the evangelist not only joined disparate sources together but composed the Gospel in a style which is consistent throughout.

5. Rudolf Pesch, *Das Markusevangelium 1. Teil: Einleitung und Kommentar zu Kap. 1.1–8.26* (Herders Theologischer Kommentar zum Neuen Testament II; Freiburg: Herder, 1976), p. 67.

6. According to Pesch, Mark inherited an early version of the passion narrative from the Jerusalem community and incorporated it into his Gospel with only minimal alterations. Pesch's theory of the pre-Markan passion narrative is the centerpiece of his second volume (*Das Markusevangelium 2. Teil: Kommentar zu Kap. 8.27–16.20* [Herders Theologischer Kommentar zum Neuen Testament II; Freiburg: Herder, 1977]). Pesch outlines his theory on pp. 1–27.

7. Paul J. Achtemeier, "Toward the Isolation of Pre-Markan Miracle Catenae," *JBL* (1970) 265–91, p. 290.

8. Paul J. Achtemeier, "The Origin and Function of the Pre-Markan Miracle Catenae," *JBL* (1972) 198–221, p. 218.

9. Heinz-Wolfgang Kuhn, *Ältere Sammlungen im Markusevangelium* (Studien zur Umwelt des Neuen Testaments 8; Göttingen: Vandenhoeck & Ruprecht, 1971).

10. *Markan Public Debate: Literary Technique, Concentric Structure, and Theology in Mark 2:1–3:6* (SBLDS 48, Chico, CA: Scholars Press, 1980). An abbreviated version of Dewey's thesis regarding Mark 2:1–3:6 may be found in her article, "The Literary Structure of the Controversy Stories in Mark 2:1–3:6," *JBL* 92 (1973) 394–401.

11. Dewey, *Markan Public Debate*, p. 1.

12. *Ibid.*, p. 110.

13. *Ibid.*, p. 119.

14. *Ibid.*, p. 167.

15. *Ibid.*, p. 195.

16. *Loaves and Fishes: The Function of the Feeding Stories in the Gospel of Mark* (SBLDS 54; Chico, CA: Scholars Press, 1981).

17. *Ibid.*, p. 103.

18. *Ibid.*, p. 107.

19. *Ibid.*, pp. 113–14.

20. *Ibid.*, pp. 40–41.

21. A similar point is made by William Telford in his intro-

ductory essay to *The Interpretation of Mark,* ed. William Telford (Issues in Religion and Theology 7; Philadelphia: Fortress, 1985). He writes, "In the case of Mark, the selection and arrangement of material and overall composition may provide a better clue to the evangelist's intention than the alterations he is deemed to have made in his source material." (p. 8)

22. *From Gospel to Tradition* (New York: Scribners, n.d.), p. 23.

23. This theory has recently been restated by Etienne Trocmé (*The Passion as Liturgy: A Study in the Origins of the Passion Narratives in the Four Gospels* [London: SCM, 1983]).

24. *The Oral and the Written Gospel: The Hermeneutics of Speaking and Writing in the Synoptic Tradition, Mark, Paul and Q* (Philadelphia: Fortress, 1983), p. 190.

25. *The Passion in Mark: Studies on Mark 14–16,* ed. Werner Kelber (Philadelphia: Fortress, 1976).

26. Werner Kelber, "Conclusion: From Passion Narrative to Gospel," *The Passion in Mark,* pp. 156–57.

27. See pp. 184–226.

28. *The Oral and the Written Gospel,* p. 215.

29. *Ibid.*

30. Ernest Best, "Mark's Preservation of the Tradition," reprinted in *The Interpretation of Mark,* pp. 119–33.

31. *Ibid.,* p. 128.

32. Ernest Best, *Mark: The Gospel as Story* (Studies of the New Testament and Its World; Edinburgh: T. & T. Clark, 1983, pp. 121–22.

33. *Ibid.,* p. 122.

34. Best makes the point, however, that "Our results therefore do not permit us in any way to conclude that in the oral period the material was conserved accurately, and naturally therefore it does not enable us to make a judgment on the 'historicity' of the material Mark preserved" ("Mark's Preservation of the Tradition," pp. 128–29).

35. Pesch, *Das Markusevangelium,* vol. 1, p. 15.
36. *Ibid.,* p. 16.
37. *Ibid.,* p. 22.
38. *Ibid.,* p. 23.
39. *Ibid.,* p. 25.

5. The Narrative of Mark's Gospel

1. Gilbert G. Bilezikian, *The Liberated Gospel: A Comparison of the Gospel of Mark and Greek Tragedy* (Grand Rapids: Baker, 1977).
2. *Ibid.,* pp. 29–30.
3. *Ibid.,* p. 30.
4. *Ibid.,* p. 43.
5. *Ibid.,* p. 76.
6. *Ibid.,* pp. 79–80.
7. *Ibid.,* p. 109.
8. Benoit Standaert, *L'Évangile selon Marc: Commentaire* (Lire la Bible 61; Paris: Les Editions du Cerf, 1983). This work is a popular presentation of Standaert's scholarly study, *L'Évangile selon Marc: Composition et Genre Litteraire.* See Chapter One, note 11.
9. *Ibid.,* pp. 35–43.
10. Vernon K. Robbins, *Jesus the Teacher: A Socio-Rhetorical Interpretation of Mark* (Philadelphia: Fortress, 1984).
11. *Ibid.,* p. 10.
12. *Ibid.,* p. 209.
13. *Ibid.,* pp. 54–55.
14. *Ibid.,* pp. 82–83.
15. Norman R. Petersen, *Literary Criticism for New Testament Critics* (Philadelphia: Fortress, 1978).
16. *Ibid.,* p. 20.
17. Rene Wellek and Austin Warren, *Theory of Literature,*

rev. ed. (New York: Harcourt, Brace & World, 1956), p. 42, quoted by Petersen on p. 28.

18. Petersen, *Literary Criticism,* pp. 38–40.

19. *Ibid.,* p. 21.

20. David Rhoads and Donald Michie, *Mark as Story: An Introduction to the Narrative of a Gospel* (Philadelphia: Fortress, 1982). Many of the conclusions from this book are summarized by David Rhoads in an article entitled ''Narrative Criticism and the Gospel of Mark,'' *JAAR* 50 (1982) 411–34.

21. *Ibid.,* p. 4.

22. *Ibid.,* p. 38.

23. *Ibid.,* p. 39.

24. *Ibid.,* pp. 59–60.

25. *Ibid.,* p. 70.

26. Petersen (*Literary Criticism,* pp. 77–78) offers a more positive explanation of the disciples' fate.

27. Rhoads and Michie, *Mark as Story,* p. 117.

28. *Ibid.,* p. 123.

For Further Reading

Achtemeier, Paul J. *Mark*. 2nd. ed. Philadelphia: Fortress, 1986.
Best, Ernest. *Following Jesus: Discipleship in the Gospel of Mark*. Sheffield, England: JSOT Press, 1981.
Best, Ernest. *Mark: The Gospel as Story*. Edinburgh: T. & T. Clark, 1983.
Bilezikian, Gilbert G. *The Liberated Gospel: A Comparison of the Gospel of Mark and Greek Tragedy*. Grand Rapids, Michigan: Baker, 1977.
Blevins, James L. *The Messianic Secret in Markan Research 1901–1976*. Washington: University Press of America, 1981.
Brandon, S. G. F. *Jesus and the Zealots: A Study of the Political Factor in Primitive Christianity*. Manchester University Press, 1967.
Dewey, Joanna. *Markan Public Debate: Literary Technique, Concentric Structure, and Theology in Mark 2:1–3:6*. Chico, California: Scholars Press, 1980.
Donahue, John R. *Are You the Christ? The Trial Narrative in the Gospel of Mark*. The Society of Biblical Literature, 1973.
Donahue, John R. *The Theology and Setting of Discipleship in the Gospel of Mark*. Milwaukee: Marquette University, 1981.
Fowler, Robert M. *Loaves and Fishes: The Function of the Feed-*

ing Stories in the Gospel of Mark. Chico, California: Scholars Press, 1981.

Hengel, Martin. *Studies in the Gospel of Mark*. Philadelphia, Fortress, 1985.

Hooker, Morna D. *The Message of Mark*. London: Epworth Press, 1983.

Juel, Donald. *Messiah and Temple: The Trial of Jesus in the Gospel of Mark*. Missoula, Montana: Scholars Press, 1977.

Kee, Howard Clark. *Community of the New Age: Studies in Mark's Gospel*. Philadelphia: Westminster, 1977.

Kelber, Werner H. *The Kingdom in Mark: A New Time and a New Place*. Philadelphia: Fortress, 1974.

Kelber, Werner. *Mark's Story of Jesus*. Philadelphia: Fortress, 1979.

Kelber, Werner, ed. *The Passion in Mark: Studies on Mark 14–16*. Philadelphia: Fortress, 1976.

Kingsbury, Jack Dean. *The Christology of Mark's Gospel*. Philadelphia: Fortress, 1983.

Martin, Ralph. *Mark: Evangelist and Theologian*. Grand Rapids, Michigan: Zondervan, 1974.

Marxsen, Willi. *Mark the Evangelist: Studies on the Redaction History of the Gospel*. Nashville: Abingdon, 1969.

Matera, Frank J. *The Kingship of Jesus: Composition and Theology in Mark 15*. Chico, California: Scholars Press, 1982.

Perrin, Norman. *A Modern Pilgrimage in New Testament Christology*. Philadelphia: Fortress, 1974.

Rhoads, David, and Michie, Donald. *Mark as Story: An Introduction to the Narrative of a Gospel*. Philadelphia: Fortress, 1982.

Robbins, Vernon K. *Jesus the Teacher: A Socio-Rhetorical Interpretation of Mark*. Philadelphia: Fortress, 1984.

Robinson, James M. *The Problem of History in Mark: And Other Marcan Studies*. Philadelphia: Fortress, 1982.

Schenke, Ludger. *Glory and the Way of the Cross: The Gospel of Mark*. Chicago: Franciscan Herald Press, 1982.

Senior, Donald. *The Passion of Jesus in the Gospel of Mark*. Wilmington: Michael Glazier, 1984.

Stock, Augustine. *Call to Discipleship: A Literary Study of Mark's Gospel*. Wilmington: Michael Glazier, 1982.

Telford, William. ed. *The Interpretation of Mark*. Philadelphia: Fortress, 1985.

Tuckett, Christopher, ed. *The Messianic Secret*. Philadelphia: Fortress, 1983.

Weeden, Theodore. *Mark: Traditions in Conflict*. Philadelphia: Fortress, 1971.

Some Commentaries

Achtemeier, Paul. *Invitation to Mark*. Garden City, New York: Image Books, 1978.

Anderson, Hugh. *The Gospel of Mark*. Grand Rapids: Eerdmans, 1976.

Cranfield, C. E. B. *The Gospel According to St. Mark*. Cambridge: Cambridge University Press, 1959.

Ernst, Josef. *Das Evangelium nach Markus*. Regensburg: Friedrich Pustet, 1981.

Gnilka, Joachim. *Das Evangelium nach Markus*. 2 Vols. Zürich: Benziger, 1978, 1979.

Harrington, Wilfrid. *Mark*. Wilmington: Michael Glazier, 1979.

Lane, William L. *The Gospel According to Mark: The English Text with Introduction, Exposition and Notes*. Grand Rapids, Michigan: Eerdmans, 1974.

Nineham, D. E. *St. Mark*. Baltimore: Penguin Books, 1963.

Pesch, Rudolf. *Das Markusevangelium*. 2 Vols. Freiburg: Herder, 1976, 1977.

Schmid, Josef. *The Gospel According to Mark*. Staten Island, New York: Alba House, 1968.

Schweizer, Eduard. *The Good News According to Mark*. Richmond: John Knox, 1970.

Taylor, Vincent, 2nd ed. *The Gospel According to St. Mark: The Greek Text with Introduction, Notes, and Indexes*. New York: St. Martin's Press, 1966.

Williamson, Lamar. *Mark*. Atlanta: John Knox Press, 1983.

What are they saying about Mysticism? *by Harvey D. Egan, S.J.*
What are they saying about Christ and World Religions?
   by Lucien Richard, O.M.I.
What are they saying about non-Christian Faith?
   by Denise Lardner Carmody
What are they saying about Christian-Jewish Relations?
   by John T. Pawlikowski
What are they saying about Creation? *by Zachary Hayes, O.F.M.*
What are they saying about the Prophets? *by David P. Reid, SS.CC.*
What are they saying about Moral Norms? *by Richard M. Gula, S.S.*
What are they saying about Death and Christian Hope?
   by Monika Hellwig
What are they saying about Sexual Morality? *by James P. Hanigan*
What are they saying about Jesus? *by Gerald O'Collins*
What are they saying about Dogma? *by William E. Reiser, S.J.*
What are they saying about Peace and War? *by Thomas A. Shannon*
What are they saying about Papal Primacy?
   by J. Michael Miller, C.S.B.
What are they saying about Matthew? *by Donald Senior, C.P.*
What are they saying about the End of the World?
   by Zachary Hayes, O.F.M.
What are they saying about the Grace of Christ?
   by Brian O. McDermott, S.J.
What are they saying about Wisdom Literature?
   by Dianne Bergant, C.S.A.
What are they saying about Biblical Archaeology?
   by Leslie J. Hoppe, O.F.M.
What are they saying about Mary? *by Anthony J. Tambasco*
What are they saying about Scripture and Ethics?
   by William C. Spohn, S.J.
What are they saying about the Social Setting of the New Testament?
   by Carolyn Osiek, R.S.C.J.
What are they saying about Theological Method?
   by J.J. Mueller, S.J.
What are they saying about Virtue? *by Anthony J. Tambasco*

What are they saying about Genetic Engineering?
by Thomas A. Shannon
What are they saying about Euthanasia? *by Richard M. Gula, S.S.*
What are they saying about Salvation? *by Rev. Denis Edwards*
What are they saying about Paul? *by Joseph Plevnik, S.J.*